The Road
to Eindhoven

First published in Great Britain in 2006 by Linthorpe Publishing, Middlesbrough.

ISBN 978-0-9553363-0-0

Designed and printed by KallKwik, Middlesbrough.

Photo credits
Front cover, Brian Spencer.

We are grateful to the following for permission to use photographs in this book. Martyn Harrison, Blades Sports Photography, Getty Images: Richard Heathcote, North News and Pictures, Middlesbrough Football Club, Highland Studios and Lauri Cox.

Thanks
Piers Mitchell of KallKwik, Middlesbrough, and Niall Kitching also of KallKwik Middlesbrough for his design skills. Proof readers, Ronnie Lynas, Mike McGeary, Dave Allan and Sarah Donald.

The Road to Eindhoven

The tale of two years, 14 countries and over 40,000 miles

By Alastair Brownlee and Bernie Slaven
with Gordon Cox

Acknowledgments

The idea behind "The Road to Eindhoven" came over a cappuccino in Rome as Bernie and I prepared for the clash with AS Roma in the Stadio Olimpico.

It was on that trip that we started to realise what a remarkable footballing adventure we were privileged to be part of and that if Boro were to reach the final then we would try to record the achievement.

On a number of occasions the rough draft was thrown in the Brownlee bin, only to be rescued after the astonishing Basel and Bucharest comebacks. Even though we were to be denied the cup by a very good Sevilla side, reaching the final was fantastic in itself and hopefully this book reflects that.

Bringing the commentary from a variety of destinations around Europe is a real team effort so I would like to thank Owen Ryan who is our boss at Century FM, Gary Weaver, Head of Sport, and technical wizard Rod Hardisty who made sure that we remained "on air".

Bernie's fear of flying means that getting him to the away destinations requires sometimes delicate handling so well done to TravelCare Sports (especially tours manager Jonathan Greaves) and MFC Travel who shared in the fun, not forgetting Graham Fordy, Commercial Manager at MFC, who organised our trips, including the rock hard bed in Xanthi! Only kidding Graham!

Naturally, the players and staff of Middlesbrough Football Club deserve a big pat on the back for making it to Eindhoven and I would like to wish Steve McClaren every success in his new role with England.

During what was at times a hectic schedule the demands on the PR department for interviews was immense so thanks to Dave Allan and his team for always saying, "Ali, I will do my best" when faced with my weekly list of players I wanted to chat to.

The UEFA Cup games ensured that I could spend a bit of time with Chairman Steve Gibson, who twenty years after helping the club survive liquidation, delighted in seeing his team go so far in Europe. As we all know, with Steve in charge there are many more adventures to come.

Gordon Cox not only works hard for the club's website www.mfc.co.uk but is also a great Boro fan and very good friend. Coxy, despite his own hectic schedule, agreed to drop everything to try and make sense of the Brownlee-Slaven ramblings. He is the main star of the book... cheers, pal.

My biggest thanks must go to my wife Wendy, daughters Alison and Emily who are always there for me and provided the hug that was definitely needed after the final. Also to my mam and dad, Mavis and Malcolm, for introducing me to the Boro all those years ago and making sure I had the right amount of euros, Swiss francs or whatever was needed for each trip.

Up the Boro!

Alastair

I'd like to thank the players, coaching staff, management and, of course, chairman Steve Gibson for making the European dream become reality.

The fans that travelled around Europe spending hard-earned cash supporting their club, especially the 32 who made each game, deserve special mention, as do the greatest supporters of them all - the disabled whose efforts to follow the team defy belief.

Also a big thank-you to Ali for nursing me through every flight and being understanding over the two games I missed. And a massive "thank you" to Gordon Cox who had the unenviable task of turning my scribble into part of this book!

A big "thank-you" too, to Gareth Southgate for writing the foreword.

Finally, an apology to both my sons, Dominic and Ryan, for failing to get them tickets for the cup final in Eindhoven.

If it's any consolation, I'd like to dedicate this book to them.

Bernie

There are only 32 fans who have been to each and every game Boro have played in UEFA Cup and I'm lucky enough to call two of them friends.

Lenny Shepherd and Nigel Gibb were among those who made their own way to Xanthi in the far north-east corner of Greece - their return journey took 26 hours and they only got back from Heathrow on the day they landed after meeting another Boro fan in Athens!

I was lucky enough to have them for company as I, literally, took the road to Eindhoven where I was fortunate enough to meet another good friend Dave Thomas, grown men sharing emotional moments.

Martin Stockton, a mate of mine for many years, once spent a sum of money he'd rather me not mention on checking Boro scores when he was working in Finland. Dave Pratt and the lads from the Sedgefield branch of the Boro supporters club deserve a mention for their outstanding loyalty, as does Ken Daly for an endless supply of information.

Life hasn't been easy in the Cox household in recent months with football induced mood swings which would test the patience of a saint. Thanks to Sarah, Lauri and Jamie for support I probably didn't deserve and to my mother who I only managed to see on rare occasions.

Thanks to Bernie and one of my best mates Ali for asking me to help them put their memories on paper.

To all those above, the thousands of fans who couldn't get a ticket for the final, and those that did, this book is for you.

Gordon Cox

Contents

if...

If you can keep your head when all about you
Are losing theirs and blaming it on you,
If you can trust yourself when all men doubt you,
But make allowance for their doubting too;
If you can wait and not be tired by waiting,
Or being lied about, don't deal in lies,
Or being hated, don't give way to hating,
And yet don't look too good, nor talk too wise:

If you can dream - and not make dreams your master,
If you can think - and not make thoughts your aim;
If you can meet with Triumph and Disaster
And treat those two impostors just the same;
If you can bear to hear the truth you've spoken
Twisted by knaves to make a trap for fools,
Or watch the things you gave your life to, broken,
And stoop and build 'em up with worn-out tools:

If you can make one heap of all your winnings
And risk it all on one turn of pitch-and-toss,
And lose, and start again at your beginnings
And never breathe a word about your loss;
If you can force your heart and nerve and sinew
To serve your turn long after they are gone,
And so hold on when there is nothing in you
Except the Will which says to them: "Hold on!"

If you can talk with crowds and keep your virtue,
Or walk with kings - nor lose the common touch,
If neither foes nor loving friends can hurt you,
If all men count with you, but none too much;
If you can fill the unforgiving minute
With sixty seconds' worth of distance run,
Yours is the Earth and everything that's in it,
And - which is more - you'll be a Man, my son!

Rudyard Kipling

Foreword

by Gareth Southgate

When we lifted the Carling Cup in 2004 it not only signalled the end of over a hundred years of hurt, it launched the Boro into Europe for the first time.

There was a notable buzz around the dressing room as we waited for the draw for our first match. Those ties against Banik Ostrava were great evenings and whetted the appetite for everybody, and over the following two seasons, to be the captain of Middlesbrough in previously unthinkable ties against the likes of Lazio, Sporting Lisbon and Roma was an honour.

At home, the 'European nights' became special occasions to look forward to - an added bounce to the Riverside atmosphere.

We loved travelling around Europe and laughed as we tried to walk around the various towns, only to be seized upon by an invasion of Boro fans, whose passion, colour and impeccable behaviour, spread a fantastic message about Middlesbrough around Europe.

Of course the end of that second year brought nights that will be remembered by those who took part - players and fans for years to come.

We sat in the dressing room after the comeback against Basel and said, 'well, you'll probably never take part in a game like that for the rest of your lives' - only for it to happen again just three weeks later!

Qualifying for the UEFA Cup Final in only our second year of European football was a remarkable achievement and whilst the end was a shattering disappointment against a quality Seville team, the journey was an incredible one.

'A small town in Europe' was indelibly marked in the history of the UEFA Cup.

1. Let's start our journey in South Wales

Alastair Brownlee

ONE Hundred and twenty eight years of hurt but we never stopped believing...

As a Boro fan it was dreamland. Gareth Southgate lifting the Carling Cup at the Millennium Stadium on February 29 2004. I was trying to blink back the tears and commentate on the historic moment for Century FM.

It had been a rollercoaster of emotion from the moment Bernie and I took our seats in the press box and the action started... Joseph Job 1-0, Bolo Zenden 2-0, but Boro never do anything the easy way and, after a Kevin Davies shot squirmed past Mark Schwarzer, it was a real nail-biter until Mike Riley blew the full-time whistle.

The strange thing was that, for a moment, we didn't know what to do... Boro had actually won. Memories were still painful of Wembley, where hopes had turned into despair, but this was different and soon Cardiff was rocking to the biggest Boro party of all-time.

A week later, and as the Carling Cup was being paraded in front of 150,000 fans on the streets of Middlesbrough, we were commentating on the scenes at the Riverside and a fan shouted up "Hey, Bernie... hope you have got over your fear of flying - it's Europe next."

Bernard Joseph Slaven turned pale, and the Euro adventure for the small town in Europe was about to begin.

2. Onwards to Ostrava

Alastair Brownlee

Middlesbrough Football Club had played European opposition before. On May 8 1908 Boro played a Danish University side away from home, winning 5-3, and on a regular basis played European sides, usually as part of pre-season training.

The first game at Ayresome Park against a team from Europe was a floodlit friendly with FC Cologne on November 13 1957. Floodlit games were still a novelty and the match attracted a crowd of 31,923, with Brian Clough striking Boro's goal in a 2-1 defeat.

The first foreign opposition I can remember came in the Anglo-Italian Cup. The tournament was designed to promote sportsmanship and good relations between the two countries... the reality was anything but as the games developed into wars of attrition with sendings off more common than goals.

My dad took me into our usual position in the Holgate End for the first tie against AS Roma on May 2 1970 and my boyhood hero John Hickton cracked in a great free-kick to win the game 1-0. Elsewhere on the pitch, Bill Gates and future great coach, Fabio Capello, in the spirit of the competition, kicked lumps out of one another!

The Anglo-Italian Cup also gave me my first chance to commentate on Boro in Europe, as under Lennie Lawrence we travelled to Pisa. Co-commentator was ref Jeff Winter and a number of Boro fans made the trip. Jeff and I shared a room overlooking the railway station and, while he was taking a morning shower the electricity went off. Jeff stumbled out of the shower and I guided him to the light and gave him a towel. As the class one referee wiped the soap from his eyes he saw that I had positioned him on the balcony and the Winter manhood was on display to the good citizens commuting around Pisa!

The game ended in a 3-1 defeat and Craig Hignett had his shirt nearly ripped off his back in another attempt to introduce a feeling of fair play and sportsmanship!

But if the European experience so far had been a hotch potch of friendlies and minor tournaments, all that was about to change as the UEFA Cup draw was made from Monaco in the lavish surroundings of the Grand Hotel.

Sadly, the budget allocated prevented Gordon Cox and I from attending, but we devised a plan of broadcasting the draw "as live" from Boro's Rockliffe Park training ground.

After a smooth introduction, the thought of Gordon and I on the terraces of the Grand Hotel was shattered by young members of the academy staff who opened the door to the office with a loud cry of "Baguette for Mr Cox"... "Room service" and a variety of other remarks concerning Coxy and I sharing a room together!

Once the serious matter of the draw started, Boro were paired with the champions of the Czech Republic, Banik Ostrava, in the first round of the UEFA Cup. The draw could have been kinder and it was clear Boro would have to be at their best, otherwise the European adventure would have a rapid ending.

Boro as a club may have been Euro novices but during the close season the additions of Jimmy Floyd Hasselbaink, Mark Viduka, Ray Parlour and Michael Reiziger meant that the squad was full of individuals who had experience of European campaigns and that would be vital, especially against Banik Ostrava.

It's the fans that make football special and in its former guise as the Inter Cities Fairs Cup the idea behind the tournament was to create good relations and trade between the cities involved. *Fly Me To the Moon* is the Boro fanzine and they received advice for Boro fans travelling to Ostrava for the second leg from a Banik fan called Miro who had his own internet site.

Unfortunately, the cost of coming to Teesside was something Miro couldn't afford so Chris Turner and other fans rallied round and paid for him and his young son, Jan, to fly to Teesside to watch the first leg. A great gesture.

The game took place on Thursday September 16 2004 and, as the team sheet was handed out, Bernie took in the names of the opposition that seemed to resemble a mixture of vowels and consonants more in keeping with an edition of Countdown.

As the game progressed, any attempt at pronouncing the Ostrava players disappeared to be replaced by reference to "the lad over there". As Boro started to open up their three-goal lead, I asked Bernie who had impressed him in the opposition to be given the reply, "the number 21, and you can pronounce it Ali... that's your job!" Cheers, pal...

As Boro's cup run developed, more and more commentaries found reference to "the lad over there," so much so that when we eventually went out to Sporting Lisbon, on the phone-in after the game, a caller said to Bernie there was one player that should be top of Steve McClaren's summer shopping list, a player who had stood out in every commentary.

"Every commentary?" asked a bemused Slaven. "Yes every one" replied the caller and after a pause said, "You know, Bernie... he's called the ladoverthere!!!"

It was comfortable against Banik once Jimmy Floyd Hasselbaink had struck Boro's first UEFA Cup goal at the New Holgate End. Jimmy's effort was followed by two from Mark Viduka, and the commentary claim of "that could be Czech mate" for once seemed accurate.

The second leg brought huge problems for the commentary team as Bernie's fear of flying was well known, and it's a long walk from Linthorpe Road to Ostrava!

Bernie had tried and failed to make flights with me before. On one occasion we were to fly to Madrid to do a TV interview with Juninho. Boro were playing at Arsenal the day before the flight and Bernie seemed to spend most of the build-up to the game in the Highbury toilet. Brian Little, who was a summariser for BBC Radio FiveLive, came up to me and asked, "Is Bernie ok these days?" I was puzzled. "Why?" Brian answered, "It's just he's in the toilet pouring tablets down his throat."

Bernie's dose of tranquillisers, designed to help him face the flight to Madrid, brought a surreal air to the commentary. As Brian Deane scored, my decibel level reached orbit. However from a near comatose Slaven the response of "yeah, Al, whatever" conveyed to the listener all was not well.

The end result was Bernie fled back to Teesside after the game and I carried on to Madrid alone... so would he make Ostrava?

The taxi to Durham Tees Valley airport was booked for 7.30... at 7.29 Bernie arrived, he had obviously had little sleep and had tranquillisers floating in the blood stream but he was here. How he had made it is his story, but he had, and all I had to do was get him on the plane!

We might not have been flying to Barcelona, Madrid or to Turin to face Juventus but no-one who arrived at the airport cared about that. The check-in desks were crowded with Boro fans and a huge cheer went up when Steve Gibson arrived.

The chairman has done so much for the club, part of the consortium that saved the Boro from liquidation in 1986, inspiring the move to the Riverside and backing his managers so that eventually the Carling Cup was placed in the trophy cabinet.

Yet, despite all that, Steve prefers to stay away from the limelight and, as he checked in, I remembered that at the moment of the club's Millennium Stadium triumph he had to be almost pushed onto the pitch to join in the celebrations. Some other chairmen would have already been on there milking the moment but that's not Steve's style.

Meanwhile, Bernie had remembered his passport and his mood lightened as he found out that his old team-mate John Hendrie was going on the trip for TV. 'H' is a great joker and just what Bernie needed.

Bernie tried to interview H once for a TV piece and it just ended in uncontrolled laughter.

John had gone on an end-of-season trip just after Boro clinched promotion in Bryan Robson's first season. Usually John's trips away ended in disaster and this was no different. After a few drinks too many, H collapsed by the pool. The players saw a chance to get the big joker back and laid him face down, pulled down his shorts and arranged the pool umbrellas so that every bit of John was covered from the raging sun... apart from his backside.

When H awoke he had sunstroke on a very delicate part of his anatomy and required an injection of steroids from club Doctor Lawrie Dunne - Doctor Dunne was a medical practitioner with a build, shall we say, on the large side. I once got into trouble for saying in commentary that he had waddled onto the pitch. Mrs Dunne waited for me at the next home game and reminded me her husband was a doctor, not a duck! Anyway, as John completed the story for the cameras, he came out with the line "Doctor Dunne, now there's a fair bum... "

Both Bernie and H started giggling and the interview had to be abandoned with tears rolling down their faces. Every time Bernie and H meet, it's to a roar from one to the other, "Doctor Dunne... now there's a fair bum!!"

Childish? Definitely, but as the greeting roared around the airport Bernie started to relax and that was just what the Doctor would have ordered.

The flight was, actually, uneventful and as we landed in Ostrava the planning of the afternoon began.

Training at the Bazaly Stadium was at 5.30 and, under UEFA rules, the press are allowed to watch the first fifteen minutes. Going to the stadium also allows you to check that everything is okay for the commentary the next day.

Ostrava is a bit like Teesside in some respects as it is an industrialised town and the steelworks made it seem as if we were around South Bank or Grangetown, not somewhere in the Czech Republic. The stadium was open on three sides with just one small covered stand where I interviewed Steve McClaren - the boss was confident but taking nothing for granted.

Included with the squad was a former team-mate of Bernie's, Colin Cooper. Colin had joined Boro in 1984, he had been through the liquidation crisis, played in the promotions under Bruce Rioch and had a second spell at the club under Bryan Robson. Now here he was training and set to play in Europe. Coops was relishing every moment and he deserved it.

After training, it was back to the hotel. Bernie joined the Legends phone-in from his room whilst I found out that there was a sauna.

Now, back at home, Bernie and I have a sauna at the Tall Trees Hotel every Thursday. It's a way of catching up on all the gossip and allows Bernie to take the mickey out of my Speedos!

So after Bernie finished the Legends we headed for the Ostrava sauna in the company of Darren Fletcher from FiveLive and H. At first we were not allowed in, the member of staff frowned and just kept pointing at our shorts. "Hey, you're not a poofter are you!" shouted Bernie and, with a shrug, the guy let us through.

I was last in and, after a spell to adjust to the dark, saw what the member of staff was trying to explain... as the naked form of everyone came into view. Shorts were not allowed! Naturally, we admired the female form but then noticed behind us were some gents... something touched John on the shoulder bringing the shout "H, I hope that's his loofer!" Cue usual laughter.

The following evening the sauna incident was relayed on Century by Bernie and, needless to say, Mrs Brownlee was not impressed.

We then set out to try downtown Ostrava with everyone set to congregate on Stodolni Street, and the majority of fans seemed to be in a pub called Bernie's Bar!

After a few lagers, cokes for tee-total Bernie, we found a pizza restaurant. Eleven of us crowded in and the owner telephoned for help. The chef arrived on a motorbike and with the press pack in thirsty mode he soon ran out of glasses. You had to keep your own if you wanted a drink.

The total cost of the meal, including drinks, was under a tenner which frustrated some of the hacks who were looking to build up the expense account!

Just before we went back, we had one last drink in another bar in the street and found Steve Gibson enjoying himself with the fans, and that's just how he wanted it to be.

The day of a game tends to be a bit of a drag if there is not a lot to see and the good citizens of Ostrava would admit it doesn't have a lot to offer, but outside our hotel was parked the Middlesbrough Disabled Supporters minibus.

Led by their chairman Paddy Cronesberry, they are amongst the best fans you will find. They had driven from the Riverside, via the ferry, to Ostrava. I asked Paddy how they had got on, to get the reply, "It was rough, we only survived Poland thanks to Red Bull and vodka!"

The minibus looked in need of a good wash but they had made it. In a small way Bernie and I had helped with their transport, as when their previous coach ran out of steam, we made an appeal to try to raise money for a new one on Century. The cost was to be £25,000 and they were struggling.

Brooks Mileson, the now enigmatic chairman of Gretna and founder of Arngrove Insurance - sponsors of the Northern League, offered to donate five grand. It was a terrific gesture and I went along to watch the presentation of the cheque at the Riverside.

Brooks asked Paddy how much more was needed. £15,000 was the reply. Brooks ripped up the cheque in his hand and wrote out a cheque for the rest.

The disabled supporters had their minibus and I always look out for Gretna's results... Brooks is a top, top man.

I am always keen to get to the ground early before any game and Boro's first away day in Europe was no exception, so a taxi was ordered to get Bernie and I to the stadium an hour before the Legends started and about four hours before kick off! Slav usually complains about being at the stadium too early but I always remind him of the late, great Bill Shankly who, after retiring from management at Liverpool was hired as a commentator by Radio City for the 1976 UEFA Cup Final in Bruges.

At 10am on the morning of the game, Shankly rang Elton Welsby, who was the presenter. "Ellie, my son, I think we ought to get to the ground early, soak up the atmosphere before tonight's big game. This is an auspicious occasion, you know."

"Fine," replied Welsby, "When do you want me to pick you up?" "Oh, in half an hour, son," replied Shankly.

Welsby picked up Shankly and, at 11am, they were in the stadium - the game kicked off at 8pm.

Shankly remains a hero of mine and if being early was good enough for him it's good enough for me.

At the stadium, Bernie and I walked around and picked up a few souvenirs before he started the phone-in. I waited for the team news in the press room, only to see tray after tray of beer being brought in. I am not sure who writes the usual Banik match report but it must be through an alcoholic haze.

Team sheet in hand, I raced to the press box only to find a silent Slaven. A local journalist had pulled his power lead out, claiming it was his socket and Czech-Boro relations seemed a bit frayed.

As the teams came out, problems broke out in the crowd. Normally, as we are there to cover the football, problems off the field are not referred to, but in this case it had to be discussed as battles broke out between the fans. Eventually order was restored but it was a reminder that, whilst we have the problem under control here, it is never far from the surface abroad.

The vast majority of the fans were well behaved and created a cracking atmosphere. The home fans erupted as David Bystron struck a great volley to give them hope. Mark Schwarzer made some great saves and when Franck Queudrue was sent off Ostrava sensed a comeback but Boro held on and, in the last minute, James Morrison raced away to score.

1-1 on the night, Boro were through.

I arrived home in the early hours. The house was quiet and whilst I was away the rewiring of the Brownlee residence had begun. I went upstairs to find the bed in the middle of the room, floorboards and carpet laid around and a note on my pillow from my wife which read, "Rewiring started. I am at my mother's, the kids are at your mother's as we can't stand the mess. Good Luck - and what about the sauna?"

Bernie Slaven

Our first game in Ostrava was a massive occasion for everyone connected with Middlesbrough FC.

This was no Intertoto, or Anglo-Italian, this was UEFA Cup football. Previous winners have included Real Madrid, Juventus, Inter Milan, Valencia and CSKA Moscow. Only three English clubs have lifted the UEFA Cup since the 70s - Ipswich, Liverpool and Spurs.

When we arrived in Ostrava I thought we were back in the Boro. It was an industrial town full of smoke and smog. Put it this way, if it wasn't for the football it wouldn't be a place you'd choose to go on holiday.

After settling into our hotel, Ali and I went for a stroll outside to stretch the legs, when out of the dusty air arrived a minibus that looked similar to the one used by Boro's disabled supporters. Neither of us could believe our eyes - it was them! Amazingly this clapped-out looking vehicle didn't look capable of making it to the bottom of Linthorpe Road, let alone a 1,300-mile trip, and that was just to get there!

We mixed with Paddy and the supporters for several hours and Paddy told us a funny story.

On the way over, the drink had been flowing when Paddy realised he had run out of tablets. Not only had he run out of pills, he had slipped and bruised himself. Anyway to cut a long story short, he ended up in a hospital and when the doctor saw his body he couldn't believe his eyes - Paddy has no legs, but he quickly assured the young doc that this had nothing to do with his fall!

I take my hat off to the disabled supporters, they've got my utmost admiration. Despite their disabilities they show tremendous courage, not just to travel and support their club, but in life in general. They're always upbeat and cheerful. Absolutely brilliant.

After chatting, Ali and I decided to go for a sauna. We were joined by John Hendrie and a lad from Radio Five, Darren Fletcher. We ventured to the Basement Hothouse. As we approached the loungers, the first guy I set eyes on was lying there with his meat and two veg on display. Instantly I thought "This is a poofter's paradise, stuff this!" But just as I was ready to turn round and head back up the stairs, I noticed his partner who was also lying there starkers - thankfully, his partner was female, and attractive at that.

Things were starting to look good. I'd been a bit apprehensive to say the least after entering the sauna and being faced with naked men. One of the lads possessed a giant loofer. Well I hope it was a loofer. If it wasn't, I'd better go and get an extension!

As we took our seats I noticed a girl shaped like a model on my right, and yes, before you ask, she was starkers. What a sight. Well, you should have seen Ali's eyes. I thought I was sitting next to Marty Feldman! His eyes were popping out of his head. I don't think Ali had ever seen a naked lady in the flesh, apart from Mrs Brownlee, of course.

If you think he gets excited watching the Boro you should have seen him in the sauna. In fact the hotel joiner had to come and dismantle the sauna box, as Ali couldn't fit through the door!

On the radio that night I made reference to Ali's exploits in the sweatbox - I heard Mrs B was none too pleased.

After cleansing our pores and stretching our groins, (our own I hasten to add) we went for a stroll and ended up in a bar called Bernie's. While Ali enjoyed refreshment inside I was posing outside with the fans. We then went for something to eat and 11 of us piled into some dodgy-looking restaurant, ordered 10 pints, a Coke and 11 pizzas.

When the bill arrived we couldn't believe our eyes, the total was £12. Astonishing, considering another 50 pints followed!

The game: We took on the Czech champions in Ostrava after we more or less buried them at the Riverside, beating them 3-0. That was no mean feat considering they were Champions League dropouts. The atmosphere inside the Bazaly Stadium was terrific, the only down note being a bit of crowd trouble involving several Boro fans. I have to say it was, in my mind, typical policing, turning up after the event!

After 20-odd minutes David Bystron hit an absolute scorcher from 25 yards which nestled into the top corner. Mark Schwarzer had no chance. Late into the second-half, 18-year-old James Morrison struck Middlesbrough's first European goal away from home. Malcolm Christie played him through and the young lad kept his cool, kept his composure and rounded the goalkeeper, a smashing finish. The game ended 1-1, Boro were through 4-1 on aggregate.

Morrison had achieved something which I would have loved to have done for Middlesbrough and scored a European goal. In fact I would have traded 50 of my goals to score one in the competition.

3. No Greek tragedy

UEFA
CUP

Alastair Brownlee

The biggest problem I think the UEFA Cup has is in the format of the group stages. Obviously it's designed to try and maximize income from gate receipts and TV revenue, but the matches are often played in front of low crowds with, by and large, the three qualifiers known before a ball is kicked.

Nevertheless, the first group game attracted interest from Boro fans, as the destination was Athens, a great city that had just hosted an excellent Olympic games, although very little was known about opponents Egaleo.

Even though it was October, the temperature was high, giving Bernie every chance to use the roof-top pool of the hotel to soak up the rays while I did the work. Steve McClaren was due to do his press conference at the hotel at 4pm and, as it was only 3pm plenty of time for a shower, or so I thought...

Wiping the soap out of the eyes, I heard my mobile ringing. It was Paul Addison of BBC Radio Cleveland. "The manager is early and wants to do the interview now, can you come straight downstairs?" Well, I have done interviews over the past 25 years in a variety of circumstances but the thought of appearing in front of the manager wearing nothing but a minidisk player was a step too far! I grabbed a towel and made it as quick as I could.

From the hotel, we made for the Rizoupolis Stadium and it has to be admitted that the ground was hardly the most imposing. Egaleo's home had a basketball court at one end with seating on one side and standing on the other two parts of the stadium. The capacity was 14,000 but the locals were of the opinion the attendance would be 3,000, at best.

Again, the media were able to watch the first 15 minutes of training, which is usually a bit of a farce as no manager wants to give anything away to watching opposition eyes and so it is usually spent playing keep-ball in a circle or jogging round the pitch.

But the bad news from training was that, after the opening session, Stuart Parnaby had fractured his fibula and would be ruled out for three months, together with the rumour that, after scoring a hat-trick against Blackburn five days earlier, Jimmy Floyd Hasselbaink would start on the bench... I will leave it to Bernie to comment on the squad rotation system but after Jimmy was made sub he did not score again until seven weeks later on December 6 against Manchester City!

Arriving back at the hotel there was a crisis underway. Boro's chief executive Keith Lamb was ready to go out for dinner and the sole of his right shoe had come off. Who says Keith is never in a flap? The solution was quickly found as Gary Thorburn - a businessman who makes the trips - knelt in front of Keith and pulled out of his pocket some glue. "Always ready for a crisis, Keith," claimed Gary and put the chief exec's footwear back together again... I wonder if Gary got a discount off the cost of his flight?

Bernie and I, together with the rest of the local media, went out for a bite to eat in the Placca area of Athens that boasts traditional Greek food in lots of good restaurants. We picked what I thought was a decent place to eat, ordered the cool drinks only to find a typical Slaven problem surface - he is the fussiest eater of all-time.

I had just sipped a lager as he announced, "Bit scruffy this, Al..." Once he had made up his mind, that was it. "My dog wouldn't eat out of here," is his usual follow-up line, together with, "If you eat out of here you will spend the match strapped to the khazi." Thank you, Egon Ronay!!

The rest of us enjoyed our food as a scowling Slaven marched off. "Just look at that," said John Hendrie. "Fussy bugger, he was just like that at pre-match meals when we were playing at Boro. He'll probably eat out of that kebab shop on the corner. Nothing wrong here, lads. Let's get stuck in."

H is spot on, Bernie is a pain when it comes to eating out but the following night at the match, just before kick off, H came into the commentary box. "Al, have you got some Imodium tablets, otherwise I might not get through the TV commentary?" Well, perhaps on this occasion Bernard was right!

The evening before the match was terrific as we were allowed inside a small ancient Greek theatre in the shadow of the Parthenon and reflected that the UEFA Cup trips certainly allowed you to see a bit of culture that you might not find wandering down Linthorpe Road!

The match itself was a bit dour until Stewart Downing came off the bench to score a terrific goal to settle the outcome. Stewart is one of us, a Boro lad, from Pallister Park, and was starting to make his mark.

Stewart had hit a terrific goal at Manchester United a couple of weeks before the Athens trip and, please excuse the cliché, as a winger he was really flying.

The Old Trafford goal had produced a piece of commentary that made me wince afterwards. "Morrison crosses for Downing to score became "Baby wonder to boy wonder in front of the Stretford End!" Naturally, James Morrison was less than impressed by the baby wonder tag the following day at the training ground, together with the nappy left in the changing room!

Stewart – sorry – Stewie has only one problem in my view, as a homegrown talent it's a lot harder to be appreciated than a player who is bought for say, five million pounds.

I had a chat with Ray Parlour, who came through the ranks at Arsenal to be a terrific servant for the Gunners, and he said that only when he left and came to Boro late in his career did he get the spotlight treatment. When Paul Merson joined Boro in 1997, he said the same. It's not a criticism of our fans but just football in general that it is harder to be appreciated when you have come up through the ranks.

Anyway enough preaching from me. As we settled into our seats for the return flight, Stewie had given our group stage a great start and it was to be Italian giants Lazio next.

Bernie Slaven

On the flight on our way over to Greece, Steve McClaren ventured up towards the back of the plane to where we were sitting.

For the majority of the flight everyone had been watching highlights of the season on the aeroplane's portable TVs. Steve told me the lads wanted to watch a video of my goals – I refused, good one. But as Steve was walking away, Ali said to me, "Slav, you should have told him it's only a three-hour flight and there's not enough time!"

When we reached our destination, Athens, the weather was glorious, at least 80 degrees. We all went to watch the pre-match training session and, before the players arrived Ali, Boro website editor Mike McGeary and myself had a kick-about on the pitch before being booted off by an angry groundsman.

On the evening, we went for our customary meal. The place of choice, in my humble opinion, was bogging, I refused to eat. When the meals arrived I was glad I hadn't ordered one. They looked like a dog's dinner. John Hendrie's steak was seeping blood, disgusting.

I disappeared and enjoyed a chicken kebab.

Around about midnight, Adam Nolan - Boro TV Ltd, Phil Tallentire - Sports Editor - Evening Gazette and I walked around the outside of the brightly-lit Acropolis, trying to get a sneak view. Unfortunately, there was a 10-foot fence and wall surrounding it.

We came to a gateway where the security guard had fallen asleep. I couldn't help thinking that at the Riverside you'd be arrested for that! Me and Ali's loud voices woke him up and he started ranting and raving in his native Greek. Although we couldn't understand a word of it we knew it wasn't complimentary. I think he was trying to tell us to f★★★ off!

We continued our walk and eventually came to the Parthenon and two burly security guards. I began by saying, "I've arrived from Glasgow and I'm due to go home tomorrow, any chance of having a look?" The answer was simple, "no, no, no."

"Come on, just a quick look?" I pleaded.

"Sorry, no."

Eventually they gave in and a quick look lasted two hours. As we entered through the archway, it led to the theatre which is thousands of years old. We sat under the starlit sky, a hot breeze blowing, chatting and admiring the spectacle, imagining what went on years ago.

The following morning we got up and headed back in the same direction. This time the Acropolis was open, but the only problem was the massive queues. We waited and eventually we were in.

On the way to the top Ali was breathing out of his backside due to his overweight frame - and the humidity, of course. I told him he should have brought breathing apparatus and, finally we reached the summit - what wonderful sights.

For me, there was only one thing missing, the Elgin Marbles. I reminded Ali that they were robbed by the British and were housed in London. "Hand them over," I demanded. Ali came out with the usual rubbish, saying, "The British took them back to the capital to preserve them, Bernard." "Bollocks," I replied.

On the evening, we arrived at the ground and I thought, "Billingham Synthonia's is as good as this." At one end of the stadium, to the left of where we were sitting, behind a goal was a solid brick wall, the width of the pitch.

I've never seen anything like it. It reminded me of playing 5-a-side indoors where you play a 1-2 off the wall.

Despite scoring a hat-trick against Blackburn, Jimmy Floyd Hasselbaink was on the bench. During my Middlesbrough career I was fortunate enough to score seven hat-tricks, but I can't ever recall being left out of the following game.

I went to see Sir Bruce earlier this year. He is now managing Odense in Denmark. I asked him the question about leaving players out when they're doing well. "Would you do it?" I asked.

"Definitely not," he replied. "It takes you all your time as a manager to get the player to a certain level. Why on earth would you want to leave him out?"

The atmosphere inside the stadium was lacking due to a sprinkling of supporters. The game itself was drab - the only bright spot was a late goal from Stewart Downing, a 20-yard effort from the inside-left position which flew across the keeper and into the bottom corner.

Back at the airport after the game I bumped into Steve McClaren. He asked what I thought of the game. I replied "average". He disagreed, then he told me he thought Doriva had had a good game. Not for the first time, we must have been at different games, because I thought Doriva was awful.

4. The lashing of Lazio

Alastair Brownlee

When the draw for the UEFA Cup group stage was made, one tie stood out - Boro v Lazio, Thursday November 4. This would be the biggest game played at the Riverside Stadium so far and the prospect of facing a big name side from Serie A had Teesside buzzing.

One player who was disappointed to lose out on facing the Italians was Gaizka Mendieta, who had signed for Lazio from Valencia for £28.9m. The move hadn't been a success but Mendieta was sidelined with a cruciate ligament injury and wouldn't get a chance to help Boro to victory.

The evening belonged to Bolo Zenden. When he first signed for Boro on loan from Chelsea, Bolo had struggled to hit form and the fans gave him some stick, but the Dutch international battled through and earned his place in the Boro hall of fame as one of the goalscorers in the Carling Cup final that had started this Euro adventure.

Bolo's first goal in front of the south stand was one of the best volleys I have seen, and his second, a header in front of the New Holgate, brought to the airwaves "Bolo has brought about the fall of the Roman Empire!"

As any listener to Century FM will know, I do tend to get carried away a bit when Boro score and I am often asked if I prepare what I am going to say in advance?

The answer is an emphatic no. While match preparation is a key part of the job, opposition players, details, match stats etc, the adrenaline rush of a Boro goal brings inspiration from somewhere. Just think of the problems if you had to try and read a prepared speech as well as describe the game. It would be chaos!

The last word on this belongs to Slav. Whenever he is asked, he replies "I never know where Ali gets the bull**** from" - and I suppose that's the ideal reply.

Six points, three goals for and none conceded represented a great start to Group E. In the Premiership, things were going equally well as Boro were up to 4th, but the toughest test was just around the corner.

5. No sweet music at El Madrigal

CUP

Alastair Brownlee

Spanish side Villarreal play in the modest El Madrigal Stadium with a capacity of just 23,000. That in itself created a problem as thousands of Boro fans wanted to make the trip and tickets were like gold dust as only 2,100 had been allocated.

We flew out to Valencia, which is about 30 miles from Villarreal and immediately set off for training. Bernie came along and, as we arrived well ahead of the team, sat in the media area pretending to be the Boro boss and fielding questions from the press. The laughter from his answers confirmed that he is better on the radio than he would be in the hot seat!

As Bernie settled to watch training, BBC Radio Cleveland's Paul Addison, Mike McGeary and I made the climb to the press box to check that our lines were in working order. But on the way back disaster struck as someone had padlocked the gate and we were now trapped in the dungeon-like bowels of the stadium.

The thought of being locked in all night with not even a dish of paella between us was a possibility until Slaven, growing worried at our absence, heard our shouts and persuaded security to let us out. He does have his uses after all!

Nights before games usually involve a bite to eat and lots of football chat. This was no exception and with temperatures at 17c it was like summer to the lads from the Boro. Valencia, where we stayed, is the city where paella was created and, with a dish of the local specialty and a glass of rioja, it was tempting to think in holiday mood, but events on the pitch the following day would bring us down to earth.

Setting out for the stadium a good five hours before kick off may seem ludicrous but Tyne Tees and BBC camera crews had to send their reports at certain times in a satellite link-up from the ground. As everyone knows, I like to get to the ground early so off we went.

As we neared Villarreal, a problem became apparent as we did our second lap of the city. The driver did not have a clue where the ground was!

Simon O'Rourke of Tyne Tees was now starting to sweat - and it wasn't just the heat. Basically, if you miss your satellite link-up that's it. Your report and pictures will not get to the studio and Tyne Tees would have a big hole to fill in that evening's schedule.

Simon's phone started to reach melt-down as his deadline neared. As we went round the same roundabout for the third time, his patience snapped, "Look, I don't know what the Spanish is for **** but he is driving this bloody bus!"

Thankfully the stadium came into view and Tyne Tees got their report with seconds to spare.

Villarreal seemed to have turned into Boro for the afternoon with about 3,500 fans making the journey and most gathered around a small park and fountain close to the ground. There was little to do apart from sing and drink beer, until some bored fans went into the local supermarket, coming out with cartons of soap powder and washing up liquid.

The local police, intrigued, gathered around and slowly realised what was going on, as from the fountain started to stream soapsuds and thousands of bubbles!!! It was the cleanest the local streets had been for years.

The game itself was a lesson for Boro. Villarreal had a good side and, in the shape of Argentinean international Juan Riquelme, possessed quality. Goals from Antonio Guayre and Javi Venta condemned Boro to their first UEFA Cup defeat and nobody could complain at the scoreline.

We headed back to Valencia, the only smile coming as a story was relayed of a Boro fan in the city the previous evening, who had, with his mate, made for a date, shall we say, with ladies of the night.

His friend crashed into the room in the establishment to find him smoking in bed with a lady on either arm. "Your lass would kill you if she found you like that", said the mate, only to get the reply, "You're right, she thinks I gave up the fags ages ago!"

Boro fans may well have scored but sadly the team had fired a blank.

Bernie Slaven

During the day of the game Ali and I did our usual tourist bit. We were in Valencia as there wasn't much to do in Villarreal, which was about 30 miles away.

We were joined by Chris Waddle, ex-Newcastle and England star. As we walked through the city centre, Boro fans shouted, "What are you doing with that Geordie b★★★★★?" Then came, "Chris, sing us that song you and Glenn Hoddle did years ago, *Diamond Lights*," and "Chris, how did you miss that penalty in the World Cup?"

We eventually sat down and had a coffee and chat, but, once again, the obscenities started flying, though in a friendly sort of way. Chris took it all in good spirits. He did tell us that if he had a pound for every time someone mentioned the penalty miss and *Diamond Lights* he would be a millionaire.

As always we arrived at the ground early. The El Madrigal Stadium hadn't opened so we went for a stroll.

I bumped into one of my old mates who told me that a colleague of his had fallen the previous night, had cracked his head on the pavement, was in intensive care and his family was having to fly out - tragic news.

Once inside the ground, the atmosphere quickly built and it didn't take long after kick-off for us to realise just how good a side we were up against.

Villarreal were technically excellent and for the opening 45 minutes we couldn't get the ball off them. They were better, quicker and had scored a fine goal.

At half-time I went to grab a drink and was surrounded by furious Boro fans. "What the f★★★'s going on, Bernie, we paid hundreds of pounds and that ginger f★★★★★'s put out an understrength team." "F★★★★★★ rubbish," added another. By the time I had listened to all the complaints I didn't have time to get my drink.

I bumped into my old team mates, Jamie Pollock and Nicky Mohan. Jamie looked like Ali's kid brother but Nicky looked as lean as ever.

Mark Viduka and Jimmy Floyd Hasselbaink came on in the second half and we perked up slightly, but Villarreal scored a second and it was good-night.

6. Pushing on past Partizan

Alastair Brownlee

The final game in Group E, against Partizan Belgrade, would decide who topped the table and, potentially, an easier tie when the competition resumed in February.

Ahead of the game in the match programme, Steve Gibson devoted time in his column to suggest that the manager should receive more credit for the work he was doing at the club. "It's now three and a half years since I appointed Steve McClaren as Middlesbrough manager. What he has achieved in that time is highly impressive - and yet I don't feel he has had anything like the praise his achievements deserve." The chairman concluded with, "So let's be proud of our manager and the success he has brought us. There is still much work to be done but Middlesbrough supporters should be shouting their praise of Steve McClaren from the rooftops."

To the outsider, it was strange that supporters and some sections of the media were slow to warm to the manager and the anger Bernie faced in Villarreal with fans upset at the team selection was a bit more than supporters who had travelled miles to watch their team lose a match.

It should be remembered that Steve McClaren inherited an ageing team, put silverware in the cabinet for the first time in 128 years, would go on to a record Premiership finish and inspire two UEFA Cup campaigns.

Probably the answer is that you only get true recognition after you leave and that in seasons to come, fans will look back with true affection for what happened in the McClaren years.

Mac is also a firm fan of the Academy system, developed so well at Boro by Dave Parnaby. After Szilard Nemeth and Joseph Job had put the side two-up, James Morrison came off the bench to score a terrific third. After cutting in from the wing he guided a fine shot into the bottom corner of the net. Baby Wonder was starting to make his own mark.

The 3-0 win saw Boro top the group, and the draw at UEFA headquarters in Nyon found Boro paired with Grazer AK with the first leg away from home in the Arnold Schwarzenegger Stadium. The Austrian's had started the season in the Champions League, losing to Liverpool, and finished third in Group F, but if Boro hit form they would be good enough to "terminate" Graz in the last 32.

7. Tight in the Tyrol

UEFA CUP

Alastair Brownlee

After the winter break, the UEFA Cup resumed on Thursday February 17 and Boro travelled to Austria with league form inconsistent since the start of 2005. Possibly the unbelievable game at Norwich, when Boro, from 4-1 up, conceded three goals in the last ten minutes, had hit confidence, but only one win in seven in the Premiership and an FA Cup exit at a Wayne Rooney inspired Manchester United had Boro in need of a lift.

Temperatures in Graz were expected to be as low as -15° so kit room assistant Elaine Profitt was sent to Argos to buy sleeping bags and hot water bottles to keep the substitutes warm. Ski shops in Boro did a brisk late winter trade as fans stocked up on boots and jackets, so much so that I was surprised the flight took off at all.

The weight in the hold might have had something to do with the strange request from the pilot just before take off. "We have a slight weight imbalance on the plane so, before we leave, the crew are going to ask some passengers to move seats." As this pre-flight game was played out, Bernie became ever more nervous and would have got off at the first opportunity. "Al," he said, "Never mind your weight, you stay at the back with me on this heap of junk."

The flight was without a hitch, but when we landed at Graz Bernie got off, grabbed his camera and shouted to a bemused Graham Fordy, Boro's commercial manager, "Fordy I am taking a picture of this and if you ever hire anything like it again you can swivel, because I ain't getting on."

Apart from a wild Scot-Irishman, the only strange sight was a lack of snow and quite mild temperatures, so all the pre-flight purchases of Arctic gear seemed a waste of hard earned cash!

Bernie and I ended up in the VIP suite at the hotel which flattered and calmed Slav down after the flight and we set out to explore Graz. Again, Bernie's eating habits came to the fore as we all ordered traditional Austrian food and he headed for a sandwich bar. But not before BBC Radio Cleveland's Paul Kerr had entered the restaurant and sat down for a bite, noticing that Graham Bell, Boro's travelling PR Officer that trip, had a bright orange top on. "Bloody hell, Graham," said Paul, "The pay's that bad at Boro, is it, that you have to double up working for Easyjet!" Cue much media laughter.

The game was great entertainment as Bolo put us in front only for Grazer to hit back. Jimmy then headed in a Downing cross to restore our lead and the Graz fans were not only bemused by the goal but also the sight of a number of our fans taking their tops off. It might not have been -15° but it was certainly nippy.

Grazer fought back to tie it up 2-2 but the funniest sight was their international striker Roland Kollman being sent off and, in great fury, kicking what he thought was protective covers around a pitchside camera. Unfortunately for Kollman, they were covering concrete and he broke his foot. Clearly in pain, he took off his boots and threw them down the tunnel. Dramatic exits don't come much better!

In the Grazer side was a tough-tackling defender... we would see more from Emanuel Pogatetz in a Boro shirt the following season as he had impressed McClaren.

The last words belong to Channel Five commentator Gary Bloom who remarked, "It will be a lot colder than this in Middlesbrough next week - it always is." Cheeky Bugger!

Boro had two crucial away goals and were clear favourites, but Bloom's prediction rang true as, surprisingly, the winter blast expected in Austria materialised on Teesside and only a heroic effort by the ground staff managed to get the game on. Grazer were less than happy when they couldn't train at the Riverside and headed for Guisborough where they trained close to the non-league side's ground, prompting their coach Walter Schachner to comment, "There must be only one snow shovel in Middlesbrough". They were a bit rattled.

February had been a good month for Boro, undefeated in UEFA and Premiership action. The match programme also paid full tribute to an event that had taken place at Villa Park on the 9th as, in the England v Holland international, Stewart Downing became the first Middlesbrough- born player to represent England since Alan Peacock 43 years earlier.

Downing played 30 minutes, wore the same number shirt as he did at Boro, 19, and kept his feet firmly on the ground. "I don't think I have made it with Middlesbrough yet, let alone England. There's so much still to work on."

Nevertheless, the left side of the Middlesbrough team - Queudrue, Zenden and Downing was amongst the best in the business and, after Grazer scored early, Downing settled the nerves by crossing for Morrison to score and, in the second half, Hasselbaink sealed the win. Boro were through to face Sporting Lisbon.

Bernie Slaven

Without doubt this was the coldest place we had visited so far. I was perished. I had taken away with me my long johns and thermal vest and I was still freezing.

Ali and I did some shopping. I think Ali bought Coxy some Schnapps, then we headed towards a massive clock perched on top of a hill. It took around 20 minutes to reach the summit. On arrival, I thought, "What's all the fuss about?"

We bumped into a couple of Boro fans and one quickly rushed away and headed for a bush. He was puking up and had no doubt overdone it the night before.

On our way down we bumped into chief executive Keith Lamb, who invited us into the Hillside Café for refreshments. Keith paid the bill. Funny, I can't remember him being so generous when he was dealing with my contracts! In fact, Keith was so tight he wouldn't give you a slide if he owned the Alps.

Bolo Zenden opened the scoring early in the second half, but Grazer equalised though Mark Schwarzer got a hand to the shot. Jimmy Floyd Hasselbaink headed in a cross from Stewart Downing, but Grazer came back to equalise.

But the funniest thing about the game was Boro's goal celebrations. Bolo and Jimmy both ran away flapping arms like some wild bird. The idea had come about when the players were shown a video of geese by the club psychologist Bill Beswick. It was some kind of motivational video. What's the game coming to? Professional footballers watching films of geese to stimulate and motivate. In my day as a player, we used to watch a porno to get us going! The game really has changed.

...enes from Boro's Carling Cup tour through the town

...ose!

The team sheet from the Boro dressing room

Visiting team
Equipe visiteuse
Gastmannschaft

MIDDLESBROUGH

To be returned
75 min before kick-off

Players starting the match	No/Nr.	Players, surnames and first names / Namen und Vornamen der Spieler	Function / Funktion	born on (DD/MM/YYYY) geboren am (TT/MM/JJ)
GK	1	SCHWARZER MARK	GK	06/10/72
	23	COOPER COLIN	CD	28/02/67
	6	SOUTHGATE GARETH	CD	03/09/70
	4	QUEUDRUE FRANCK	CD	27/08/18
	25	MORRISON JAMES	LB	25/05/86
	7	BOATENG GEORGE	CM	05/09/75
	20	GHIDGNI DORIVAL DORIVA	CM	28/05/72
	8	NEMETH SZILARD	LM	22/07/64
	19	DOWNING STEWART	F	05/08/11
	32	ZENDEN BOUDEWIJN BOLO	F	15/08/76
	21	PARNABY STUART	F	19/07/82
	14	MENDIETA GAIZKA ZABALA	F	01/08/74
Captain	11	CHRISTIE MALCOLM	F	11/04/79

Substitutes	No/Nr.	Surnames and first names / Namen und Vornamen	Function / Funktion	
GK	12	NASH CARLO	GK	13/09/73
	29	MCMAHON ANTHONY		24/03/86
	26	BATES MATTHEW		10/12/86
	31	WHEATER DAVID JAMES		01/02/87
	28	TAYLOR ANDREW DEREK		27/08/87

Officials on the substitutes bench	No/Nr.	Surnames and first names	Function / Funktion
1		MCCLAREN STEPHEN	MANAGER
2		HARRISON STEPHEN	COACH
3		BARRON PAUL	COACH
4		ROUND STEPHEN	COACH
5		MOSELEY CHRISTOPHER	PHYSIO
6		SMITH ALEX	KIT MAN

The team sheet from the Banik Ostrava dressing room

Tituaires
Antangsaufstellung

	No/Nr.	Noms et prénoms des joueurs / Namen und Vornamen der Spieler	Function / Funktion	geboren am (TT/MM/JJ)
GK	22	MARTIN RADOSLAV RAŠKA	GK	31/10/77
	2	RADOSLAV LATAL	CD	06/01/70
	6	DAVID BYSTRON	CD	18/04/82
	1	MARTIN ČIŽEK	CD	09/06/74
	8	PAVEL BEŠTA	LM	02/10/82
	14	LIBOR PAPADOPULOS	RB	14/04/85
	17	ZDENEK POSPĚCH	RB	14/12/78
	16	JOSEF DVORNIK	CD	23/04/76
	21	MIROSLAV MATUŠOVIĆ	CM	02/11/80
	23	MARIO LIČKA	F	30/04/82
Captain GK	18	ANTONIN BUČEK	F	24/02/84
	3	PETER DROZD	F	12/11/73
	45	DAVID KOTRYS	F	03/06/77
	25	JOSEF VELKOBORSKÝ	D	19/11/76
	26	LIBOR ŽŮREK	D	14/07/78
	27	ADAM VARADI	F	21/11/79

Officials	No/Nr.	Surnames and first names	Function / Funktion	
1		FRANTIŠEK KONKÁŘSKÝ	COACH	
2		PAVEL HIGALIK	ASSISTANT	
3		DUŠAN VRTO	ASSISTANT	
4		JOSEF JAROSLAV	ADMINISTRAT.	
5		HUDY TOMAS PAVLIŠKA	DOCTOR	
6		LADISLAV KRABEC	MASSEUR	30/04/65

Substitution of players	OUT No/Nr.	IN No/Nr.	Minute
1			
2			
3			

rnie and John Hendrie with friends? Well that's a first.

of these is Marty Feldman, the other is Alastair Brownlee after an Ostravan sauna -
decide which is which

Bernie tries the hands-on approach with former Liverpool star Phil Thompson

Alastair outside the Parthenon in Athens

...nie with Chris Kamara

...e with Chris Waddle

Bernie with John Hendrie inside El Madrigal

Bernie with Nicky Mohan (left) and Jamie Pollock inside El Madrigal

t to right, Eric Paylor, Alastair, Bernie high above the Austrian city of Graz

fully not what's on offer inside!

Alastair in Lisbon

There wouldn't be a second half to this book if this save wasn't made

8. Sporting suicide

Alastair Brownlee

The home leg with Sporting proved a cruel lesson in European matches. As McClaren said afterwards, "Switch off for a few moments and you can be out." The painful moments were a 17 minute spell in the second half as Barbosa, Liedson and Douala made it three-nil.

Joseph Job's spectacular overhead kick was voted the greatest goal ever scored at the Riverside and a late Chris Riggott effort did, however, give a glimmer of hope for the second leg.

Bernie and I arrived at Durham Tees Valley airport for the trip to Portugal for the second leg more in hope than real expectation that Boro could do it, but by the time we arrived in Lisbon I had convinced him we were going to do it. Or he might have just said that to get some peace.

Craig Hignett was on the trip as a summariser for FiveLive and life is never dull with Higgy as we picked a restaurant by the River Tagus to discuss the game.

There was about 12 of us as we ordered and, after an hour, although the drink kept coming, very little food had arrived on the table. A further hour later and more alcohol on empty stomachs forced a decision - we were leaving.

Unfortunately, as some snacks had been eaten, the restaurant staff insisted on the bill being paid. A diplomatic incident was brewing up, with raised voices in Portuguese and English. Eventually Higgy won the day. "I want to see the manager," said our Scouser and from a restaurant a few doors down, the manager arrived.

He then disappeared into the kitchen and came back for the showdown.

"I must apologise," were his opening words, "My chef is laid drunk in the kitchen. That is why you did not receive your food." The crisps in my hotel snack bar now seemed very inviting, despite the cost!

Lisbon is, however, a terrific city and the warm spring sunshine the following day saw Boro fans decking the main square with flags and banners. Optimism was starting to grow.

Bernie and I travelled early to the Jose Alvalade Stadium, a ground that had been used in Euro 2004 and the seats were painted in such a way that even when the ground was less than the 50,446 capacity it still looked full.

Boro played really well. Joseph Job had some chances but in the end a Pedro Barbosa goal put paid to our first UEFA Cup campaign.

The memory for me of that night is young full back Tony McMahon, who had given everything, hobbling off injured and asking the fans to try to lift their voices one more time. McMahon, together with Adam Johnson and David Wheater, all Academy boys making debuts as we just ran out of bodies.

The manager led the players to the terrific supporters at the end and a cry of "Steve McClaren's red and white army, " was heard. The manager deserved it and, perhaps, Steve Gibson was getting his wish after all.

Once you have enjoyed a taste of European football you want more. To finish the first campaign at the last 16 stage was a great achievement but could Boro qualify again?

The answer would lie in the outcome of one penalty kick, seconds from the end of the final game of the season at Manchester City.

Bernie Slaven

When we arrived in Lisbon the one thing I wanted to do was visit the Estadio Nacionale where Celtic won the European Cup back in 1967. Unfortunately we were nowhere near it and none of my pals that day, Ali, Craig Hignett or Dave Allan gave a toss.

We went for a walk down towards the sea, the evening weather was glorious. We were searching for a fish restaurant and, when we arrived, we were faced with a difficult choice. There were over 60!

We eventually picked one and around 15 of us ordered. An hour later the starters arrived. Well, some of them. Two hours later and there was still no sign of the main meals. The majority of the party became restless and headed for the exit, very frustrated and hungry. Ali and I stayed put, praying our own food would turn up.

If it didn't I was worried Ali would turn into a cannibal and start eating me. Finally the meals arrived and the lads who had left returned. By all accounts the delay was down to the cook who was lying pi★★ed in the kitchen! Afterwards Ali and I did well to escape the thousands of Boro fans who were well-oiled and enjoying themselves.

I have to say the Jose Alvalade Stadium is a very impressive arena. It's the first stadium I have seen with multi-coloured seats and, despite it being empty when we arrived, it looked as though there were thousands in due to all the different colours. Maybe we should try it at the Riverside (only joking).

It was a far superior performance from the Boro than we had witnessed at the Riverside. They knew what they had to do, trailing 3-2 from the first leg and they went chipping away, looking for that elusive goal.

Unfortunately a couple of chances went begging, Joseph Job the biggest culprit, and late on Sporting rubbed salt in the wounds.

This was our first time in a European competition in our 128-year history and to reach the last 16 was a good achievement.

Not only did Sporting end our European dreams, they went on to end the dreams of our north east rivals Newcastle, so the story had a happy ending after all!

9. Simply stunning in the City of Manchester

Alastair Brownlee

It was the ultimate in football drama. Stuart Pearce had turned around City's fortunes and, under his management, they had got to the brink of a UEFA Cup place. Boro travelled to the City of Manchester Stadium for the final game of the season knowing a point would give us, not City, the final place. It was that finely poised.

Jimmy Floyd Hasselbaink's brilliant free-kick gave Boro the lead and I remember talking on air with Coxy at half-time. He felt Boro would be OK as long they didn't concede early in the second-half – they did, through Kiki Musampa.

Boro hung on and, into injury time, Stewart Downing saw his shot saved and the action switch to the other penalty area. Stuart Pearce had gambled by putting his goalkeeper, David James, as centre-forward. It nearly paid off as a cross was aimed for James and the ball went out for what seemed a corner. But the City keeper had seen something and so had referee Rob Styles.

The ball had been deflected by the hand of Franck Queudrue... PENALTY.

It was a simple equation.

If Robbie Fowler scored, City were in the UEFA Cup, but if Mark Schwarzer saved, it would be Boro.

After what seemed like an eternity, the ball was on the spot, Fowler advanced and... "Get in, get in you big Aussie... Mark Schwarzer saves left hand side... Mark Schwarzer magnificent... Mark Schwarzer, he's the greatest Australian hero since Ned Kelly..."

People even now come up to me and tell me what they were doing when they heard the commentary. One shop assistant from ASDA said she saw a customer pushing a trolley listening to the radio suddenly leap up and start hugging other shoppers. The commentary was placed on e-mails and ringtones as Boro fans celebrated Europe.

But was Ned Kelly a hero? I said to Mark Schwarzer that I could only think of two Aussies, Ned Kelly and Rolf Harris, so I think I picked the right one and I had seen a film about Kelly that portrayed him as a Robin Hood-type figure. Anyway, the last word to the big Aussie, "Alastair, you always do go over the top, I expect nothing else – and I expected to save the penalty as well."

Well done, you big Aussie!

10. Here we go again

Alastair Brownlee

When the draw was made for the first round of the UEFA Cup 2005-06 and Boro were paired with Greek side Xanthi, a cheer broke out at the training ground which quickly turned to a groan when it was realised that Xanthi was a border town close to the Bulgarian/Turkish border – and not the Greek island of Zante that is an idyllic holiday destination!

Nevertheless we were out to improve on the previous season's place in the last sixteen, not top up on the sun tan, and in the Xanthi squad was a player who had been part of the Boro side that played some wonderful football in the rollercoaster season 1996-97, but on the down side lost two cup finals and suffered relegation.

Emerson was set for a Riverside return.

Emerson signed for Boro in the summer of 1996 from Porto for £4m and made an instant impact with his midfield strength and ability to score special goals. But his disappearing acts saw him as much on the front pages as the back of the tabloids and, on one occasion an exasperated Keith Lamb said Emmo could "rot on the beach" if he did not come back to Teesside.

I remember interviewing Bryan Robson at the training ground when Emmo had gone AWOL yet again. Robbo had his back to the window as I spotted Emmo walking, as if nothing had happened, onto the training pitch.

"Bryan, Emerson's just behind you," I said and got the response "Aye good one, do you expect me to fall for that?"

"But he is," I carried on, and eventually a reluctant Robbo turned round, saw the wayward Brazilian and yelled out of the window. "Emmo... what the **** do you think you are doing? Get your arse in this office now!"

I leave the rest to Robbo. "I was ready to give Emmo a blast but he came in with that trademark big, beaming smile on his face giving it 'Morning gaffer', and to him it was as if nothing had happened. I was ready to give him a right rollicking but in the end I couldn't because he was all smiles - that's the type of lad he is."

Sadly, it was all potential unfulfilled at Boro for Emerson. He made just 53 league appearances, scored nine goals, including a spectacular 20-yarder at Sunderland's Stadium of Light. He stayed for the start of the season after relegation, when Juninho and Ravanelli left, and his partnership with Paul Merson had Boro top of the table by Christmas, certainties for a Premiership return, but he made the disappearing act one time too many and left for Tenerife.

The question was would he be back on Thursday September 15?

He was and, although, at 33 he was a slightly fuller figure, he got a warm reception from the crowd of just over 14,000, many of whom still believed that the team he played for that crazy season 10 years before was the best ever.

The current Boro team were simply too strong for Emerson and co. George Boateng scored the first goal of the new campaign and Mark Viduka added a second. With, just as important, a clean sheet, Boro were favourites to progress.

The second leg brought about the chance of Bernie doing an Emmo and going AWOL. Slav's fear of flying has been well documented and he had done really well so far to conquer it, but the trip to Xanthi involved, potentially, on the return journey a stopover in Birmingham as the team were playing Aston Villa on the Sunday. It was the thought of landing at Birmingham and taking off again for Teesside that freaked Bernie.

As it turned out, we flew straight back, but at the time that wasn't known and so, off the subs' bench, came John Hendrie, with the plan being for Bernie to link in from the Century studio and watch the game on a TV monitor.

So it was H alongside me on the plane and, as we arrived in Xanthi, although the locals were friendly it was clear this was no holiday destination. Graham Fordy had scouted the town ahead of the trip and found only two decent hotels. The team stayed in one, the media the other.

Usually I assess the comfort level of the hotel bed by throwing my battered case on it to test for softness. In Xanthi it landed with a solid thump and, outside the window in the scrapyard, a cockerel began to crow... this was to be an interesting trip!

I have to offer sincere praise here to the 82 Boro fans who made it, despite the fact there was no official trip. Planes, trains and automobiles, all were used to get the fans there, some making a week of it, others needing 29 hours to get back to Teesside after their return flight from Athens was cancelled!

The out-of-town Xanthi arena had access by a single-track road and with stands on three sides, did not look the best. Capacity was 7,000 but next door was an excellent training complex that had been opened by Pele and included a hotel that most of the Xanthi players stayed at for home games. Clearly Emerson did not fancy the luxury of our hotel or the cockerel!

Xanthi's PR officer, Babis, was really helpful handing out a full team strip to the visiting press. I just hoped he didn't expect us to play. His brother ran a restaurant in town where we could have an excellent meal at good prices... now what was that phrase, beware of Greeks bearing gifts?...

The restaurant was fine and Boro's press officer that trip Dave Allan stood up, slightly fuelled by the local Ouzo, to give a speech thanking the Xanthi media department and friends who had joined in the meal and suggested that all the Boro media chip in for our hosts' food.

Silence reigned as journalists looked for blank till receipts, until Dave, with an extra gulp of Ouzo, rang Keith Lamb to ask if the club would contribute to the evening.

To a huge cheer, Dave announced, "The Boro would like to thank our hosts and travelling reporters. The meal is on us!"

Much food and local beverages later, Dave received the bill, settled it, and we met up with the chief exec in a bar on the way back. "Thanks very much, Keith... here's the bill." Keith took one look, winced, and replied, "Dave, treat it as salary deductable." Dave turned a pale colour, Keith smiled... I think he was joking!

Spending time with friends in the media certainly lets you into their personal strengths and occasional weakness. Adam Nolan, who runs Boro TV Ltd., producing all the club's DVDs, snores like a bull. Ross Marshall, who is the TV editor - and brilliant at the job - was sharing a room with Adam. After the attempts at strangulation failed, he resorted first of all to sleeping in the bath and then, as the noise hit a crescendo, on the floor outside the room. It was like a scene from a farmyard, Nolan bellowing one side and the cockerel the other!

On the serious side of the trip, the PA announcer did his job in the arena to perfection and the 5,013 crowd seemed to be at least six times the number in noise level. But, after a few scares, the game petered out into a goalless draw. A job well done and the group section awaited. There was just one formality to be completed.

As after every tie, two players from each side had to complete a drugs test. One of our player's chosen was the number 2, Abel Xavier.

Abel had been signed as right-back to replace Michael Reiziger and the 32-year-old Portuguese international seemed to fit the bill with bags of experience. The match in Xanthi was the fifth in succession for Xavier; his next against Aston Villa would be his last.

FIFA suspended Xavier from all competitions following a positive test on his urine sample. Xavier protested his innocence and, in a statement, he said, "I am convinced that there is a reasonable and entirely harmless explanation for such a finding." To date, none has been forthcoming.

Bernie Slaven

This was the first European trip I had missed and it was down to my flying phobia. I heard in advance that on the way back we were landing at Birmingham to drop off the team, then going on to Teesside, due to Boro's game on the Sunday against Aston Villa.

Instantly, I informed Ali and my gaffer at Century, Owen Ryan, that I wouldn't be going and that they had better get a replacement. John Hendrie went in my place and I linked in from the studio.

People often ask me about my flying phobia. I have always been frightened of flying. I drove past Lockerbie the day after the air disaster there in 1988 and since then I have never been the same.

I remember under Bruce Rioch missing a trip to Bermuda and disappearing from a London hotel in the middle of the night. I remember missing Republic of Ireland games, telling Colin Todd to ring Jack Charlton and report that I had the flu. I've paid for holidays myself, got to the airport and about-turned.

Anyway, I remember watching this game from the studio. As a spectacle it was awful, but we got a draw and that's all we needed.

11. Getting past the Swiss guard

CUP

Alastair Brownlee

The first group game would see Boro travel to Switzerland to face Grasshoppers Zurich and Bernie was back in flying form.

On the flight, Steve Gibson came down to join Bernie and I and asked if he could go on the Legends Show as, with the Premiership season spluttering, there had been a bit of flak flying around from the fans and the chairman wanted to meet it head on.

The night before the game seemed out of the question as Bernie uses the phone in his bedroom to do the first half hour while I am at training. I know Steve and Bernie have a great relationship but the thought of them sharing Slav's bedroom might have put that under strain so I suggested we do it the following night before commentary. It would also enable Century and Boro's official website www.mfc.co.uk to "trail" the appearance and maximise the audience. I was pleased when that was agreed.

Grasshoppers' Stadium had a rather weary feel to it and a bit of uncertainty was put in my mind when a local journalist mentioned that they had some fans who would be out to cause trouble. I said when remarking on the trouble in Ostrava the previous season, in England we have battled hard to rid the game of the hooligan element but, sadly, abroad it still exists as some Boro fans would find out in Zurich.

The evening before was pleasant enough with Keith again picking up the media evening meal bill and the press lads given a long, tiring walk around the city only for our leader, Graham Bell, to admit having the map upside down!

The following day I spent some time with Bernie doing an interview about his career that would run on the *Soccer Saturday* programme I host on Century when Boro don't have a game.

I had recorded chats with Eric Gates and Malcolm MacDonald previously and now it was Bernie's turn, which would also help publicise the launch of his book, *Legend?*

The book would be a big Christmas hit and go on to raise over £32,000 for the Ann Charlton Lodge in Redcar for sufferers of MS. It was a typical gesture from Bernie. Many ex-stars might have said a donation will go towards the charity but not Slav. He visits Boro fans who supported him when he played and this was his way of supporting them when they needed it.

The interview also reminded me of how far the club has come in 20 years. When Bernie signed we played at Ayresome Park, a ground that was once great but had fallen into decline. He was housed in digs opposite where I live now (the sweet wrappers are still under the bed!) and the club faced a financial crisis that would lead to liquidation.

Thanks to the man who would appear on the Legends, we now play in a top class stadium, are established in the Premier League, have won the first major trophy in 128 years and reached the final of the UEFA Cup in just our second year in the competition, and yet Steve Gibson was facing fans' discontent... amazing to the outsider.

It is, however, probably true that if Bernie wrote to Boro in 2005 as a striker from Albion Rovers in need of a trial he might not get the same response he received in 1985 and would be left cutting grass in Glasgow, not scoring 147 goals for Boro. You just wonder how much fate plays a part in a footballer's career.

I set off for the ground with Gary Gill, who also played his part in the club's post '86 revival, and Paul Addison. It was, as always with us, early and gathered around the entrance were some Grasshoppers "fans" who probably would not avoid trouble if it came along. We were relieved to get inside the ground and set up in the press box.

Before kick-off, the sound of sirens could be heard outside the stadium. Boro fans who had arrived were on one side of a tramline, the same side as the Grasshoppers ultras. Unfortunately, a tram arrived leaving the police on one side and the fans on the other. The Grasshoppers hooligans seized their moment and attacked the Boro supporters. When the tram pulled away the situation was inflamed by the police indiscriminately firing rubber bullets at anyone in the way. It was chaos.

Luckily, no-one was badly hurt but here was another reminder that what we exported in the dark days of the eighties to the continent is still in certain areas very much alive.

I did a chat for Century with Superintendent Steve Swales of Cleveland Police, who was in Zurich with his colleagues, as they are for all away matches, and he was just relieved no one was hurt and compared the style of policing abroad, which seems to be stand back until you have to act and then go in hard, with ours which is more proactive.

On the field, Jimmy Floyd Hasselbaink scored a well-deserved goal and Boro, as we had a year previously, started the group stage with a 1-0 win.

Bernie Slaven

On the plane on the way over to Zurich, the King of Teesside, Steve Gibson, came to the back for a chat. Nearing the end of our conversation, Steve asked if there was any chance of coming on the Legends show. I replied "Of course" and suggested he did it the night before the game. Ali thought it would be better doing it from the stadium before the match and after a discussion with Gibbo, that was agreed.

We arrived at our hotel and the trip got better. I wasn't rooming with Ali as I had been on some previous trips. I mean Ali's a great guy, my mentor, my mate and my father figure, but when it comes to sharing a room, he's the last guy I would pick.

He farts, snores and talks in his sleep and he's up at six in the morning gargling, shouting and singing. He's a nightmare!

The following evening, we headed to the stadium on the press bus, had a good journey and everything worked inside the ground. We linked into Gatesy for the Legends show - thankfully Supermac was off, so the show was slicker, quicker, with no hint of sarcasm.

For two hours solid the show was hijacked with Boro fans all wanting to have a chat with the chairman. The one thing I had warned Gibbo beforehand was that none of the callers were vetted, he would have to take them as they come. "No problem," he replied.

The calls came fast and furious and Gibbo replied with great honesty and warmth. The one thing about the chairman is that he has never forgotten his background. Coming from Park End, he speaks the same language as the fans and the paying public appreciate him and adore him for that.

He sailed through the broadcast and came out of it with his crown in tact. Don't forget, this was at a time when things weren't going well on the park. He didn't have to do it.

He left his place in the commentary box and took his place in the directors box, Ali sat down beside me and we started the commentary on the game. The broadcast had worked like clockwork - well, it was Switzerland I suppose.

Again Mac had made changes, four from the game against Portsmouth the weekend before. He knew what he was doing, as we started well, with Mendi nearly scoring with a free-kick from just outside the box.

But we didn't have long to wait as Jimmy Floyd Hasselbaink scored after nine minutes rounding off a great move with a low shot from a few yards inside the box.

Grasshoppers thought they had scored after Schwarz had fumbled a shot from Rogerio and Eduardo put in the rebound. He was offside, but the move and 'goal' had given the home side heart. We came under a lot of pressure and Eduardo headed wide while my Gran could have headed in a chance Scott Sutter missed 10 minutes from half-time.

Gran would have had another had she been given the chance Dos Santos had just before half-time. He shot over from six yards. Gran would have put it in while making a pot of tea.

We were better in the second half. Viduka might have scored twice on another occasion, Eduardo headed over, while Doriva should have passed to Viduka who would surely have scored, but he shot for goal. Now, I would never have done that...

Rogerio went close late in the game, but Boro held on and the fans were in full cry with one of their songs which would soon become famous, "Geordies at home, watching The Bill."

12. Dniproblem

Alastair Brownlee

Our second group match came just after a great Riverside performance, as Manchester United were thrashed 4-1. It was the ideal preparation for the arrival of Dnipro from the Ukraine but, for me, a slight disappointment.

Bernie always makes a point of my rose-tinted spectacles combined with my devotion to the team and I always put a pound on Boro to win every home game 4-0.

Before the match, Bernie was crowing, "Well, Ali has done it again, 4-0 to Boro," he announced to the listeners. "He should be locked up!"

With 60 seconds to go, my bet at odds of 100-1 had the smirk wiped off Slav's face and a lovely Sunday lunch treat was lined up for the Brownlee household... one Ronaldo header later, Mrs B was back cooking the lunch. It was still a great win though!

The attendance against Dnipro was just under 13,000, again, in my opinion, underlying the need for UEFA to revise the group stage. Boro were never in trouble against disappointing opposition.

Yakubu and Mark Viduka (2) sealed the win and Boro began to plan for what could be a table-topper decider against AZ Alkmaar, and Bernie got out his plan of Amsterdam!

13. How far is Amsterdam?

Alastair Brownlee

It was a short flight to Amsterdam from Teesside and walking through Schipol airport reminded me of a pre-season trip in the Robbo years.

Arriving in Holland, all the players made their way to passport control including Hamilton Ricard. At immigration, Ricard realised he had forgotten his passport and still tried to wander past the checkpoint. Imagine the chaos as a six-foot plus Colombian tries without a passport to avoid customs!

Ricard was escorted to a detention room as Robbo said, "Let's get the lads to the hotel, Ham has some explaining to do."

The club had to arrange to fly out Hamilton's passport before he could enter Holland... let's hope the body search wasn't too painful!

Thankfully, our arrival was a lot smoother and we were soon in Alkmaar.

They are building a new stadium on the outskirts of town but the current ground could only accommodate 408 Boro fans, with tickets therefore highly prized amongst the Boro supporters and many expected to travel without.

Alkmaar was one of the clubs where Jimmy Floyd Hasselbaink had started to make his mark as a player and he also knew their coach Louis van Gaal very well. This match would be tough.

The training session went smoothly and the squad seemed in confident mood.

Before leaving for Holland, Steve McClaren had agreed a new deal tying him to Boro until 2009 and Steve added, "I want to get the message across that I am absolutely committed to Middlesbrough Football Club. We have enjoyed success in the last four years and I want to be even more successful in the next four."

The only slight problem, as revealed by Keith Lamb on the Legends in January, was that the physical signing of the contract hadn't taken place. That was rectified in 2006, but begs the question where is a pen when you need one?!

So to the evening's entertainment. Wisely, Paul Addison and I decided to stay in

Alkmaar and enjoyed... a Greek restaurant. As for Bernard, he can account for his behaviour elsewhere.

The following day was drab and grey. We had a look around town and I set off back for the hotel at about midday to take a bite to eat and do some prep on the opposition for the commentary.

Bernie stayed in town under the excuse he wanted to buy a chandelier! And I thought it was cheese you brought home from Holland.

About 90 minutes later, I had just finished a shower when I heard a voice in the corridor, "Al, Al, where are you?"

I opened the door and there stood Slav, out of breath, looking as if he had stood under a waterfall.

The reason? "It started to rain, couldn't get a taxi so walked back. Halfway back, it was p***ing with rain, I needed a pee couldn't find the loo so went up a wall. Some woman came out with an Alsatian and set the dog on me, I just ran back as quick as I could. Good job I didn't buy the chandelier."

Some explanations defy both logic and belief.

The game was played in a torrential downpour. Brad Jones, deputising for Mark Schwarzer, made some great saves and Boro survived everything that Alkmaar could throw at them. It was the first time AZ had failed to score at home in six games and the goalless draw secured Boro a place in the knockout stage with still one game to play.

After the match, I headed down to do the post-match interviews and, as it had been an early kick off UK time, left Bernie to do the Legends. I was just at the bottom of the stairs if there were any problems and, in seconds, I could help.

Anyway, after interviewing Brad Jones, Chris Riggott, Mark Viduka and Steve Gibson about the draw, I arrived back to what was a deserted commentary position to find a note... it read:

"Ali.

"The line went off, I'm p***ed off and I've f***ed off to the press room.

Slav."

So, if you were a Legends caller that night, my apologies with the rider... never give a boy, man's work.

Bernie Slaven

We travelled to Alkmaar, but the question on everybody's lips was, "how far's Amsterdam?"

The game was on the Thursday, so on the Wednesday night four of us jumped in a taxi for a journey which took 45 minutes, before arriving in the red light district. Their names will remain anonymous to protect the guilty.

I have to say I thought we were in the centre of Middlesbrough. It was a sea of red and white. There were Boro songs coming out of the local bars and queues of Boro fans waiting to see their favourite girls.

The place was buzzing. We bumped into several of the disabled supporters, just like we had in Ostrava. They were well-oiled and enjoying the scenery.

As always, several dodgy looking guys approached us asking, "Would you like Charlie?" When I was in Amsterdam years ago, I thought they were saying, "Do you know Charlie?" Charlie, in case you don't know, is a drug.

We continued to admire the sights when one of the lads went missing. He soon returned with an alligator smile. No need to ask where he'd been.

We arrived back at our hotel in the early hours of the morning. The guy who had disappeared was scratching like a monkey. No doubt he'd caught something.

Later that day, after a good night's sleep, I went shopping and left Ali behind. On the way back I couldn't stop a taxi so I walked about 40 minutes in the pouring rain. When I arrived back at the hotel I was like a drowned rat. I headed straight for Ali's room, looking for a bit of sympathy. When he opened the door, posing in just his floral boxer shorts, I didn't know who looked worse.

It was a good night for fishing.

The rain poured, but there was a great atmosphere in a ground which only held 9,000. This was Alkmaar's last season at the Alkmaarderhout Stadium. Next season they're moving to a ground not far away which will hold 30,000.

Alkmaar had a goal chalked off for offside and we continued to battle and scrap for everything. We didn't create a great deal, but 0-0 was a good result considering the previous season had seen Alkmaar reach the semi-final of the UEFA Cup and we had matched then on their own turf.

At the end of the game, for the first time in 10 years, Ali left me in control while he went to get some interviews. I linked in with the Legends, but after about five minutes the line went dead. Some b****** had pulled it out, and do you know what? I haven't got a clue how to reconnect.

I hung about like a lonely man on the streets of Amsterdam. I gave it 20 minutes and thought "F*** this." I was freezing, the rain was bucketing down, the stadium had emptied and there was no sign of Ali.

So I left him a note, which I think he has told you about on another page!

I finally caught up with him and jumped on the coach to the airport for our flight. While queuing to get on the plane, Mark Viduka (The Duke), somehow ended up with the press. I've met The Duke on several occasions. We shook hands and had a good old chat.

Ali asked him, "Have you heard Bernie on the radio?" The Duke replied, "His nickname is Simon Cowell, yeah, that's his job." I asked The Duke how he coped with the squad system. I said I had watched him being a regular with Celtic and Leeds.

He replied, "What do you want me to do, knock the manager's door down?" I said the thing he was missing was that if he hadn't scored 20 goals by the end of the season the fans would look at him as a failure. I said they'll not look at games where you've been injured or rested, they'll look at your tally.

He half agreed.

14. Levering Litex out of the way

Alastair Brownlee

The final game in Group D came against Litex Lovech with Boro requiring a win to confirm their place as group winners, therefore giving a potentially easier tie in the last 32.

Not too much was known about Bulgarian football but, in my research, I found out that after leaving Boro Hamilton Ricard played in Bulgaria, so clearly he found his passport after all.

In a pre-Christmas fixture the match attracted the first sub-10,000 gate for a home UEFA cup tie but we should praise the 9,436 who made the effort to see a terrific double strike from Massimo Maccarone clinch a 2-0 win. Both goals came in the last ten minutes... was this a sign of late Maccarone heroics to come?

15. No Stuttering

UEFA
CUP

Alastair Brownlee

After the winter hibernation the UEFA Cup began again for Boro with a difficult tie against top German side Stuttgart.

The intervening months had been tough; a 7-0 defeat at Arsenal and a 4-0 reverse at home to Villa had brought massive pressure on McClaren and his chairman. A lesser chairman would have wielded the axe, as a fan, summing up the mood, threw his season ticket at the manager and the Riverside seemed in revolt.

"Now is the winter of our discontent, made glorious summer by this son of York." William Shakespeare - *Richard III.*

Well, this son of York, Steve McClaren, had a lot of work to do to dispel the clouds around his management, but seven days after the Villa debacle we defeated Chelsea 3-0 at the Riverside, so perhaps the gloom was starting to lift as we flew to Stuttgart for the away leg of the last 32 tie.

The drizzle that greeted us on arrival couldn't stop the laughs. Curtis Fleming, who was deputising for Gary Gill on BBC Cleveland, and Gary Pallister, who was on duty for Channel 5, joined Bernie.

Bernie made the first howler seconds after landing, "Look at all those planes over there," he said pointing at the Lufthansa aircraft. "You can tell you're in Germany, everywhere you look it's the bloody Luftwaffe!" Now, if we had said that?

The trip to the hotel was fraught. Bernie had lost his phone, the hotel itself was ill-prepared for Slaven's arrival - see his views on his loss of footwear -so I made a sharp exit to watch training.

The Gottlieb-Daimler Stadion has a capacity of 51,165 and was upgraded to become a venue used in the 2006 World Cup.

It is a great place to watch football, apart from the running track that surrounds the pitch. Nevertheless, the upgraded floodlights were excellent, making training seem as if it was in daylight, and so were the press facilities.

I had a real buzz about the game as I sent my interviews back to Century.

We headed back to the hotel ready for a German lager and a bite to eat before the big day.

Stuttgart, as a city, was a little disappointing. There was a clock counting down to the World Cup in the main square and footballs in the trees but it just seemed a bit tired.

The Boro players came out of the hotel for a pre-match walk and signed autographs for the fans. As the clock ticked towards kick-off, we set off for the stadium.

Initially, we weren't, despite all of our accreditation, allowed in, and only after being referred to six stewards we were eventually let inside. Goodness knows how they coped when faced by press from around the world.

However, once inside with the lights shining brightly, it became a magical venue for football and the adrenaline started pumping... or at least until 30 minutes into the Legends when they decided to evacuate the stadium to test procedures for the World Cup!

Quite why the powers that be decided on a UEFA Cup night to tell everyone to leave the stadium beggars belief, but faced with a row of stewards shouting, "Out! Out! Out!" in a manner last seen in *The Great Escape*. Bernie made his apologies to Supermac and Gatesy, and left.

Halfway down the stairs, we were told we could go back. So much for German efficiency.

The game itself got off to a great start, Jimmy Floyd Hasselbaink, a rejuvenated striker in 2006, scored the opener, although Century listeners were denied the usual Brownlee yell... the line to our studio had gone down the second Jimmy struck.

I spent a frantic 10 minutes trying to restore it and eventually we got back on air, but it was one of those moments when you panic, shout abuse at the equipment and, if all else fails, pray that the line will be restored.

Thankfully it was, as Stuart Parnaby grabbed a second and, despite a late Stuttgart strike, we had a great 2-1 away win.

On the way back came a classic Ross Marshall moment. A member of the press remarked how much he had enjoyed visiting the Porsche museum in Stuttgart. "Did you hear that?" said Ross. "How can anyone enjoy a museum about something you put on the front of the house, that must be really boring." We creased up. Good job Ross is the best editor in the business, as the rest of life seems to swim by.

If we thought the tie was over, then we were in for a shock at the Riverside. Stuttgart clearly still believed that they could turn it around and, after 13 minutes, Christian

Tiffert's goal added to the visitors' confidence – one more goal and they would be heading for Rome, not Boro.

At tough moments, you turn to the skipper for inspiration and Gareth Southgate answered the call as he has done so often. Steve McClaren's first signing, and generally regarded as his best, Southgate marshalled the defence with Chris Riggott alongside him to thwart all Stuttgart's attempts to score and, although at times it wasn't pretty, it was 'job well done' and we made it to the last 16.

The final thoughts on a dogged Riverside display belong to Gareth. "Just a few weeks ago we might have folded – as we did against Villa following an early goal, but we grew as the game went on. Our season stays alive."

Bernie Slaven

On the way to Stuttgart I had a chat with Stewart Downing in passport control. I said I thought he should be in the England squad. He disagreed, he thought Kieran Richardson should be.

We touched down safely in Germany and I had a quick chat on my mobile while I was still on the plane. Distracted, I got off the aircraft and got on to the wrong coach.

When we finally arrived at the hotel, I discovered I had lost my phone. Things went from bad to worse.

We went for a sauna and, when we came out, my shoes had disappeared. Instead of two size 9s being where I left them, there was a pair of size 7s with holes in them. I thought "Some bastard's at it." I put on my dress shirt and trousers and went looking for the manageress.

I started ranting and raving, "These are not my shoes, someone has switched them." She was shocked. I honestly thought some German had taken mine and replaced them. Not only had they switched shoes, they had switched socks as well.

After getting no joy from the manageress, I jumped into the lift to the ground floor and marched out with no socks and shoes on. The lads were in stitches. The on-looking residents in the five-star hotel were far from amused.

It turned out that Adam Nolan had hidden my shoes and the pair he had replaced them with had been abandoned by someone. I'm not bloody surprised, because Steptoe wouldn't have worn them!

When we arrived at the stadium you could see why it had been selected for World Cup games.

After being hemmed in for the opening 20 minutes, we scored a smashing goal through Hasselbaink, totally against the run of play.

In the second half, George Boateng found himself on the right wing and his delivery was met by Stuart Parnaby, who guided it into the top of the net for our second goal.

Stuttgart scored after Fabio Rochemback conceded a free-kick, but it was much too late for the home side, who were still getting used to a new coach after Giovanni Trapattoni had been sacked leading up to the game.

16. A Roma Therapy

Alastair Brownlee

To say that Roma would represent the toughest test yet on the road to Eindhoven would be an understatement.

The Serie A giants had just set a record 11 successive league wins, the eleventh win made all the sweeter as it came against local rivals Lazio. Although the sequence came to an end with a 1-1 draw against Inter Milan, they were in peak form.

Unfortunately for Roma, but a bonus for Boro, their club captain and world-class player Francesco Totti had broken his ankle against Empoli the previous month and was ruled out for the rest of the season.

Another factor in our favour was the Riverside pitch which was clearly showing signs of wear and tear, so much so that Roma coach Luciano Spalleti remarked that it was the worst surface he had seen. So perhaps if the coach was a bit unsure that might get through to his players.

Boro got off to a terrific start as keeper Gianluca Curci charged out of his goal, fouled Hasselbaink and referee Alain Sars had no hesitation in awarding a penalty. We had played only 12 minutes...

Yakubu placed the ball on the spot and then coolly slid the ball in one corner as Curci dived the other way.

Roma pushed for an equaliser but McClaren's tactics were spot on as he used Hasselbaink in a withdrawn role to effectively man mark Olivier Dacourt. This stifled the Italian's creativity and a defence so frail in the opening months of 2006 again stood firm.

Andrew Davies was living a dream. After being out on loan to Derby, he was recalled in January and was now in the heat of a UEFA Cup campaign at right-back.

"To play for Middlesbrough, my hometown club, in European ties is amazing. Going out on loan made me mentally stronger and I am enjoying playing at right-back, which is a new position for me. The Roma game proved that in Europe you have to work the ball much more, not give it away, and I think we have a great chance of going through."

As the full-time whistle blew, Dava had good reason for his optimism - a clean sheet, a one-goal advantage and all to play for.

So all roads led to Rome for the 3,500-strong red army. As usual the players and media flew out the day before the game and, as Mac gave his pre-match interview in the surroundings of the Stadio Olimpico, it was hard not to pinch yourself just to believe that Boro really were here to play for a place in the quarter-final of the UEFA Cup.

I had been here before, as a fan, for the European Championships of 1980 as West Germany beat Belgium in the final. The Boro supporters club had organised a Beeline coach trip from their offices in Linthorpe Road to support England and to take in the final itself.

The finals were marred by crowd trouble in Turin and we were subjected to teargas and heavy handed police tactics, but the S reg coach made it to Rome via games in Turin and Naples, eventually returning to the Boro with more miles than an Apollo spacecraft!

A lot had happened in the intervening 26 years and surely the policing tactics would be much improved?

The events of the evening reflected badly on the underlying problems of hooliganism that is still rife in Italian football. Boro fans, young and old, were enjoying a peaceful drink in one of the many squares in the Italian capital when they were set upon by a gang of Roma ultras wielding an assortment of weapons including knives and axes. According to Boro supporters, many of whom fled in terror, the police presence seemed to be downgraded just before the organised attack.

The only relief in a horrific incident was that no-one was killed, although three fans had been hospitalised, one of whom remained in hospital overnight.

Gary Philipson used to be our touchline reporter at the Riverside, but had taken up duties with TFM as a late-night talk show host and his programme had fans ringing in giving graphic accounts of what had happened. It all sounded terrifying.

The following day Superintendent Swales briefed the media at our hotel stressing that this was an unprovoked attack on Boro fans and the overall impression was relief that the Boro fans had not been more seriously hurt.

I spent much of the day filing reports to our news team so it wasn't until quite late in the afternoon that the Evening Gazette's Eric Paylor, Dave Allan and I enjoyed a walk to the Colosseum and Roman Forum. Even there the phone still rang. I was getting my photo taken with the Roman centurions when the mobile rang. "Sorry to trouble you, can we have a quick update on what's going on? You're live on the news in 30 seconds."

Goodness knows what the centurions made of it, 2,000 years earlier I would have probably been thrown to the lions.

Everyone gathered together outside the hotel for our journey to the stadium at five o'clock UK time. The previous evening, the journey had taken 20 minutes. All the press piled on the bus, reflecting that we would be in good time and Bernie could do the Legends live from 6pm.

The journey, as many Boro fans found that night, turned into a nightmare.

We arrived at the main entrance within 100 yards of the media zone only to be told that we did not have the right bus pass to be let in. We then undertook, with a police escort, a detour that involved nearly colliding with a tram, doing a u-turn in six lanes of motorway traffic and our frustrated coach driver eventually driving at speed past arm-waving stewards to get in to the stadium.

The whole journey lasted nearly two hours and we arrived back at the stadium 50 yards from where we had started!

It was a relief to settle into our seats in the press box. The Boro fans were to our left and the curva sud, with the noisiest Roma fans, to our right.

They certainly know how to create an atmosphere. Just as I went on air, a huge thunderflash cracked through the ground. I remarked that the last time so much gunpowder had been gathered together Guy Fawkes was in charge.

As our fans were having small items, including the ever-dangerous lipstick, taken from them, the Roma fans seemed able to let off at will flares and explosions.

On the field the Boro grabbed a vital away goal 12 minutes from the break as Stewart Downing, watched by Sven-Goran Eriksson, crossed for Jimmy to power his header past Curci. The curva sud fell silent. I raised my voice high in celebration, as a member of the Italian press also seemed aware of the goal as he slowly raised one finger in my direction.

Sadly, just before half-time, Mancini scored. With 65 minutes showing, Ray Parlour fouled Okaka in the box... penalty... Mancini scored again. Now it was real pressure. One more Roma goal and we were out, but keeper Mark Schwarzer was magnificent.

In January, transfer-listed at his own request, it seemed as if his nine seasons at Boro were about to come to an end. But he stayed, worked hard, came off the list and showed in Rome what a world-class keeper he is.

After what seemed like an eternity, the full-time whistle blew. We were through! On Century, it sounded as if I was in tears. Well, it was a bit emotional and the sight of the players celebrating in front of the fans brought a lump to the throat.

The only downside was that the fans had to wait two hours before being allowed out of the Stadio Olimpico. In advance, Adam Nolan had put together some highlights of previous games to show on the electronic scoreboards. The fans enjoyed the show, especially the trail for Bernie's DVD! In his hour of triumph, Mac saw Bernie on the big screens and heard cries of, "Bernie, Bernie, show us your arse!" The manager looked up at the press box, smiled and shook his head.

On the pitch, Chris Riggott asked Gareth Southgate what it was all about. As Gareth continued his warm-down the words, "Riggs, don't even go there," summed it up!

Back at a pizza bar close to the hotel the food tasted great, but one stat clouded the win. George Boateng and Lee Cattermole had been booked, meaning both our central midfielders would miss the first leg of our quarter-final (we didn't know at that stage who we would play).

Cattermole had only made his Premiership debut at Newcastle on January 2 and, 12 months before Rome, faced a long time out with a tear to his lateral knee ligaments. Now he was making his mark at the top. The night against Roma was special, as he commented, "It was the highlight so far. My friends and family were at the match and I could pick them out in the stands. The last 20 minutes were as tense as anything I have known and the atmosphere was terrific."

Lee would be missed in Switzerland, as 2006 was turning into the year of the Catt.

The final word on Rome came from Superintendent Swales as I interviewed him at the airport before the flight back. "A very large number of fans travelled and were well behaved, no arrests were made. They did not rise to the provocation and I would like to thank them for that."

In Italy, it had been a team effort on and off the pitch.

Bernie Slaven

Of all the places I've been around the world, Rome is definitely one of my favourites. To go to Rome and watch my beloved Boro in action in a European game was a dream come true.

Previous visits included 1990 when I was part of the Republic of Ireland squad for the World Cup finals. I had the great fortune of meeting Pope John Paul II, sadly he's now passed away. The only downside of that trip was Italy knocking us out of the competition in the quarter-finals.

The next visit was some nine years later when I travelled there to meet Fabrizio Ravanelli. The White Feather, as he was known, was playing for them at the time.

But the visit with the Boro was the real deal. We departed Durham Tees Valley Airport an hour late due to Arctic conditions with plenty of snow. So much so that the wings had to be de-iced before take off. Not good for my nerves.

On arrival, Ali, as always, headed to the stadium. I went to the hotel to link in with Gatesy and Malcolm for the Legends show, after which I just had a quiet meal and went to bed.

I set the alarm for 8am and I reckon I was the only member of the press who was alcohol-free. Before leaving the hotel, I left several notes under Ali's door to let him know my whereabouts, only to find out later he didn't receive them as I had put then under the wrong door!

I went to do the tourist bit. First visit was St Peter's Square. The sunshine was glorious and I stood along with thousands of others waiting for the arrival of the newly appointed Pope Benedict.

After an hour, he past me in his unguarded Popemobile. I was five yards away and attempted to take several pictures with my camera above my head. I flicked through them with great anticipation, wondering what I had snapped. When I looked I had several excellent pictures of a woman's headscarf!

After the Vatican, I went to the Trevi Fountain, which was surrounded by Boro fans. The sun was still glorious. The saying goes that if you turn your back to the fountain and throw a coin over your head and make a wish you shall return to Rome. I had done this years earlier and here I was back in Rome.

Just as I was about to throw my coin I couldn't believe my eyes. There was a woman with a long cane with a magnet on the end, and do you know what? She was fishing the money out! Cheeky bitch. Her partner seemed to point to the coins that were magnetic and she would fish.

I made sure my coin landed in the middle, only to be told by a Boro fan that she could still reach it as she had an extension!

Time to move on. Next stop, briefly, was the Spanish Steps then a quest to find the favourite hotel and café of my idol, the singer Morrissey.

Amazingly, within 20 minutes, I had discovered both. This Mozza has been a resident of Rome for the past year, staying in the Hotel De Russie. When I arrived, there were limousines galore parked outside with mafia-style chauffeurs.

There were at least three doormen guarding the entrance. I gained entry and had a good look around, admiring the décor and inhaling the aroma of fresh cigar smoke.

I considered having a pot of tea and a sandwich, but when I had a look at the prices my appetite soon disappeared. Next I wanted to find out where Morrissey's favourite café was.

Inside Café Greco, I found a modern bit and a part which dated back to 1760. The waiters were dressed in tails, very posh indeed. I enjoyed a coffee and flaked tuna sandwich then headed back to my hotel, La Griffe, to prepare for the game.

The reason Ali hadn't come sightseeing was because of the trouble in the city the night before. He had to do bits and bobs for the radio on the events, which were sickening by all accounts.

Boro fans had been drinking in a bar when smoke bombs were thrown in and gangs of Italian yobs ran in, wielding machetes. Several Boro fans were injured.

We departed for the game with a police escort, only to get to within 10 yards of the stadium gate and be told we had to go to another. The delay in getting there was farcical and I was late for the Legends show which was disappointing.

Inside the stadium, an abrupt steward asked me to produce my ticket. As I pulled it out of my pocket, he grabbed it off me. Abruptly I returned the compliment and gave him a filthy stare. He was in the presence of two girls, maybe he was trying to impress them.

I took my seat and finally linked with the Legends show. It was amazing that we were taking calls galore from agitated Boro fans who were sat on coaches waiting to come to the game. They were stranded in some local park, concerned they wouldn't make kick-off.

The stadium was half empty. Nevertheless, there was still a great atmosphere. Roma started the better side and missed a couple of gilt-edged chances.

Totally against the run of play, Downing produced a magnificent cross for Jimmy Floyd to score with a fantastic header. All in all, it was the start we had dreamt of - a world-class ball and finish.

Roma came roaring back and grabbed two, but the required third was denied by excellent defending and brilliant goalkeeping. Mark Schwarzer's heroics were reminiscent of the great Russian goalkeeper Lev Yashin.

At the end of the game, the players and management ran to the 3,000 Boro fans who had made the journey. Those fans were locked in for two hours to avoid confrontation with the Iti's. To keep them occupied, screens at either end of the park started to show Boro's 3-0 drubbing of Champions Chelsea in February.

After the Chelsea clips, I couldn't believe my eyes. As the players were in a circle warming down, on the screen was an advert for my forthcoming DVD. Up came Bernie Slaven to music. Next, "147 goals. The Legend?" God knows what the players and management thought. Next came action of goals scored by me. I have to say I was embarrassed.

After the footage, I could see Steve McClaren looking up towards me as if to say, "What the f*** was all that about?" The fans started chanting, "Bernie, Bernie Slaven," then "Bernie, Bernie show us you arse," ending with, "Offside offside, offside offside."

Eventually, the fans were given the all-clear and they departed dreaming of the next round.

17. Rolling the Swiss

Alastair Brownlee

The quarter-final had Boro paired with FC Basel, with the promise of a semi-final against either Rapid or Steaua Bucharest if we could overcome the Swiss champions. The first leg was away from home. That caused a logistical problem for Graham Fordy when he tried to book accommodation, as at the same time as the game, the town of Basel was hosting a jewellery and watch fair which is the biggest of its kind in the world. The nearest hotel Graham could book was in Zurich, one and a half hours away. This promised to be a tiring trip.

As the aircraft's descent began for Basel, an announcement was made from the flight deck, "Good luck to the team in tomorrow's game and let's hope Bernie Slaven gets a hat-trick!" Bernie went a shade of red and dashed for his seat. I haven't seen him move that quickly in years. There was a collective shaking of heads among the management team and the responsibility for the announcement will be left hanging, as we were, in the air.

On arrival in Basel, I set off for the stadium and Bernie departed straight for Zurich so he could join in the Legends.

With time tight, the idea was for Steve McClaren to do his pre-match chat at Durham Tees Valley Airport before we left. That would have enabled us to go straight to the press box in Basel, send our reports and get on the coach for the journey to Zurich. Unfortunately, on arrival at the stadium we were told we couldn't go into the press box until after McClaren had done his press conference for the Swiss journalists, so all our time-saving efforts seemed in vain.

Graham Fordy pleaded to let us in, trying every way he could to alter the Basel press officer's mind, all to no avail. Graham eventually stormed off, muttering, "We'll make them stand in the Riverside car park next week!"

Eventually, we gained access and, with the clock ticking sent our interviews. It seemed as if the Swiss were making life a bit difficult, but this was the last eight, so it was serious stuff now.

On the journey to Zurich, I had a chat with John Murray of BBC Radio FiveLive. John is a great broadcaster and someone I have known since the nineties. John came to BBC Radio Cleveland as head of sport when John Allard, who had given me my big chance, left. It must have been tempting for John Murray to take over the Boro commentary. He had been doing it for TFM and it is the fun part of the job, but he kept faith with Gordon Cox and I, for which we were grateful.

When John left for a position with the Beeb in London, he championed my corner to take over from him as head of sport, but that summer Century FM won the exclusive Boro commentary rights. I faced a dilemma. At the time I had a full-time job working for Barclays Bank. Did I give that up to work for BBC Cleveland, covering other teams and sports but giving me a BBC career path? Or did I accept the 17 pounds per game offered by Century to be the co-commentator with Dave Roberts and Big Malcom Allison?

At Century, initially, it would be like going back to square one where I started with Cleveland in 1981.

The answer came from Mrs B, "You are a Boro fan. What would you be thinking if you were at Darlington or Hartlepool and Boro were about to kick off?" Wendy was right and I accepted 17 pounds per game.

John and I had a great chat, as he was looking forward to working on the World Cup in the summer, and the following day we were all going to FIFA headquarters for a meal, together with a chance to see the World Cup. I joked to John that if Sepp Blatter was in, he might as well pick up his press passes and see if he could get me on the list for the England games!

After a draining day, a meal at the hotel and bed would have been great but the club laid on a bus to the centre of Zurich for the chance to have a walkabout. Bernie and I found a restaurant we had used prior to the Grasshoppers game. I sent a text to Gary Weaver, Century's head of sport, asking what we could afford in the budget as the menu was expensive, and back in October, Keith Lamb had settled the bill. The reply, "Boro in the quarter finals... budget gone long ago... enjoy... good job Bernie doesn't drink!"

Matchday, some of the media set off early for Basel and asked if I would put their bags on the coach when it set off later in the day. I said "No problem", but gave them Bernie's room number to stack them outside. An ever-furious Legend kept hearing a knock on his door and bags appear in front of his room and, in the end, to the shock of the chambermaids, ran naked down the corridor, chasing the latest person to put their luggage at his door... not a pretty sight!

FIFA Headquarters was an interesting experience as the building is set at the end of an innocuous row of houses but, as the drive and buildings open up, has a great view of Lake Zurich.

The meal was excellent and the Jules Rimet Trophy is still gleaming!

I purchased a miniature copy of the World Cup to Slaven's, "That's the nearest you will get to winning it, Ali!"

Every major tournament we have the same ritual. He comes round my house to watch the game, I ply him with food and coke, he says, "Ali, I want you to win, my kids are English," and then cheers the opposition and smiles when we get knocked out!

"Well, this summer will be different," I thought as I clutched my World Cup. "Just don't drop it on Rooney's foot," said Slav, as I paid for it... I think I should ask him for the lottery numbers.

In football, you sometimes get a premonition about a match and, for whatever reason, whether it was the travelling or the loss of Boateng and Cattermole, I felt uneasy - and that's not like me. Bernie sensed it, as he said, "Well, prediction, pal?" I replied "One-nil." Slav replied, "I think I need to take your temperature," but something did not feel right. This was no time for my usual 4-0 prediction.

The pre-match concerns materialized as Matias Delgado hit a shot that Chris Riggott seemed to duck under, it bounced wickedly in front of Mark Schwarzer and Basel led 1-0, 43 minutes played. Two minutes later, David Degen raced through to double Basel's advantage.

Basel had not lost a league game at home for three years and tried to end the tie, but Riggott made a terrific goal line clearance. Ugo Ehiogu nearly scored just before the end but the saddest sight of the second half was a dreadful facial injury to Emanuel Pogatetz that was to rule him out for the rest of the season.

All in all, an awful night. After the match, as I waited outside our dressing room, the Basel team were singing. They had completed a lap of honour at full-time and certainly that wound up our players. Bottle it up and use it at the Riverside, I thought.

The flight home was a subdued affair and, at Durham Tees Valley, as we waited in the rain to enter the terminal building, surely an ambulance or a car could have collected Emanuel Pogatetz, who was pushed in the rain past the fans through passport control. Emanuel was clearly in pain and it made a sad picture as he was wheeled through... it just summed up the whole bloody trip.

So a two-goal deficit and without an away goal, Boro were clearly on the UEFA Cup ropes, but the boss hadn't given up on it. "No-one is under any illusions about the task ahead but the belief and the desire is there - and the prize could hardly be greater. If we pull it off it will arguably be the greatest night in the Riverside's history and one that will be talked about for generations."

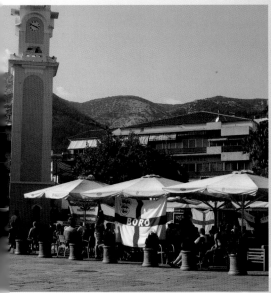

…ro fans in Xanthi

Chairman of the Middlesbrough Disabled Supporters Association Paddy Cronesberry, right, with two friends in Xanthi.

…too much more would be seen of Abel Xavier after Xanthi

Alastair and Bernie have just missed their tram in Zurich.

A fashion boutique named after Bernie in Zurich? Probably not…

Not a sight many would want to see!

chairman Steve Gibson, left, with Bernie during the 3 Legends phone-in on Century FM

Alastair with the World Cup

The closest a Scotsman will ever get to football's greatest prize!

rnie in the Gottleib-Daimler Stadium, home to VfB Stuttgart

Rochembach in action against VfB Stuttgart's Silvio Meissner

There are many captions which could go with Bernie, Botty and Rome

Bernie in Saint Peters square outside The Vatican

orrissey

e pretending to be Morrissey

Alastair in the press box at the Stadio Olimpico, home to AS Roma (and Lazio)

Jimmy Floyd Hasselbaink heads Boro into the lead in the Stadio Olimpico

Stewart Downing

Gareth Southgate

Pardon the language! It lost nothing in translation and was soon removed.

Bernie with BBC Cleveland's Gary Gill

...oadcast equipment used all over Europe by Ali and Bernie, photographed here in Basel

...imo Maccarone scoring against FC Basel at the Riverside

Opposition™

If you're a trouble-lover, you'll be enthralled by the many exotic ways in which the police and other state institutions can make your life a hell including:

- one weekend at Jilava, the most famous jail
- apartment in a old communist block of flats
- negative press for you all the time (including when you are doing something good for the country)
- party offered by your business partners with bribe episodes
- salvaging populism and mass adulation
- provoking inter-ethnic conflicts

Warning: the opposition of the government can lead to adverse manifestations to your health or /and that of your bank account.

For those wanting the ultimate **Opposition**™ package, each customer has a comprehensive range of All inclusive facilities included in the price. Details on the web page.

Governor™

A laid back lifestyle with all the ingredients for a most spectacular holiday with a winning combination of governing position including:

- one weekend at Cornu, the famous VIP residence
- protocol luxury villa
- positive press for you all the time (including when you are implicated in a scandal)
- for a minor extra charge we can guarantee even a NUP (the police will drop the investigations in your case)
- bodyguard driver and car with siren and lights bar
- party offered by your economical partners with bribe episodes

Warning: the opposition of people masses can manifest itself under the form of eggs and tomatoes.

For those wanting the ultimate **Governor**™ package, each customer has a comprehensive range of All Inclusive facilities included in the price. Details on the web page.

...ademy manager Dave Parnaby, with Alastair and Eric Paylor in front of the palace once used by ...tator Nicolae Ceausescu

...to right - Alastair, Colin Cooper, Curtis Fleming in Bucharest

The atmosphere builds in Bucharest

Massimo Maccarone scores Boro's late, late winner against Steaua Bucharest

...areth Southgate

...o right – Mark Viduka, Massimo Maccarone, Doriva in Boro's dressing room

Kitted out by Bakers Tailoring of Linthorpe Road, Middlesbrough

The world's largest parmo cooked by Joe Rigatonis of Linthorpe Road in Middlesbrough

If Mac still believed, so did we... let battle commence.

In front of 24,521 at 8pm the second leg started.

1 min Yakubu shot wide.

23 min Eduardo scores 0-1, aggregate 0-3. It seemed all over.

33 min Viduka scores with a crashing drive.

56 min "GOOOOOAAALL." Viduka scores 2-1. Boro, Agg 2-3.

79 min The Hasselbaink hammer...' "You beauty, Jimmy!" 3-1, aggregate 3-3 – but Boro still trail on the away goals rule.

And now enter the gladiator... Maccarone had been brought on in the 67th minute as McClaren threw caution to the wind, four up front.

Maccarone, Viduka, Hasselbaink, Yakubu.

It was a throw-back to the "old days", 4-2-4, but it was effective and Boro had hope, but the clock was ticking against them.

Into the last minute, Rochemback hits a shot, Basel keeper Pascal Zuberbuhler parries, it falls to Maccarone, who takes aim and...

"It's in, it's in, Massimo Maccarone has scored for the Boro! The Gladiator has struck and Boro have come back from the dead. My eyes do not believe what I am seeing. This is the greatest comeback since Lazarus!"

The press box, like the rest of the ground, was going wild. But hold on, Eduardo races clear. Surely not heartbreak? Mark Schwarzer pushes it wide for a corner that was cleared, and pandemonium reigned as the whistle blew.

"The Swiss have rolled! William Tell, Heidi, the lot of you, Boro are in the semi final!"

Whilst a delirious commentator felt as high as the Transporter Bridge, the skipper summed it up. "Winning the Carling Cup was a huge moment for Middlesbrough and all the players who were involved. But to win a UEFA Cup quarter-final in the way we did puts that match right up there among my all-time most memorable games," said Gareth Southgate.

Bernie Slaven

The usual early morning flight was put back to 1.30 in the afternoon, which made me a bit more uncomfortable, having more time to think.

About half an hour before landing, I ventured from my seat at the rear of the plane to have a chat with Graham Fordy, commercial manager, and Jane Woods, ticket office gaffer.

As I sat there, a feminine-sounding voice came over the tannoy system. "I'd like to wish Middlesbrough Football Club all the best tomorrow night against Basel and I hope Bernie Slaven gets a hat-trick!" My first thought was, "That b★★★★★★, Ali, has stitched me up again." I felt myself getting lower in my seat and the conversation came to an abrupt end.

I got up and marched to the back of the plane in Hitler fashion. Right away, I pointed the finger at Ali. He instantly proclaimed his innocence, but all the press started laughing.

Before I knew it we had landed and we now had to find our way to the hotel. As I was waiting for my bags, I chatted with Steve Gibson about games past and games coming up, and our annual trip to Singapore in May.

Although we had landed at Basel, there were no rooms in the city due to a cuckoo clock convention. Therefore, we had to travel for well over an hour to a hotel in Zurich.

When we arrived, we did the usual ritual. Ali went to the stadium to find out where he was going to put his wires (for the radio broadcast) and I linked in with the Legends from the hotel.

On the evening, Ali and I walked through the cobbled streets of Zurich like a pair of lovers looking for an eating place. Eventually, we found the place we were looking for. We'd been there in October when we'd played Grasshoppers.

We hung around the hotel the following morning after breakfast waiting for the bus, which was to take us to FIFA headquarters where the club had arranged lunch and a tour.

FIFA HQ was perched on the top of a hill. The view was breathtaking, it was just a pity it was raining heavily.

Lunch consisted of a four -course meal which included FIFA salad with eggs, bacon and croutons, seared fillet of beef in a red wine sauce, sauté potatoes with truffles, followed by chocolate cake and orange sauce. For once, even I couldn't complain.

Afterwards we went in search of the World Cup, which I told Ali England were not going to win in the summer, and the cup they did win in 1966. We found both and they looked stunning in their brightly lit glass cases.

After the tour, the bus dropped the majority of us off in the town centre. Ali and several others headed for the stadium and I met up with him there.

Away to our right inside the ground was a massive banner which stretched almost the width of the stand. On it were the words, "Beat f*****g Boro, win the cup tomorrow." I couldn't believe my eyes. How on earth do you get into a professional ground and be allowed to display something so crude?

At the Riverside we can barely get in with a Middlesbrough-crested flag – unless it is an official flag night, of course. Haha!

For the opening 35 minutes of the game we were comfortable. We didn't look in any danger. Then, bang-bang we were two down in two minutes. The half-time whistle soon followed and we were like the 2,000 travelling fans, stunned.

Reflecting on the goals, for the first, Gaizka Mendieta made a half-hearted challenge on the halfway line, Ray Parlour looked like he was treading water as he was easily beaten. Matias Delgado struck a shot, Chris Riggott, for some unknown reason, ducked, the ball bounced before it reached Mark Schwarzer, left the Aussie in a heap and Basel were 1-0 up.

For the second, they just tore us apart down the inside right channel. David Degen left Emanuel Pogatetz for dead with his pace and Schwarzer was disappointingly beaten at his near post.

We defended better in the second half and rode our luck, Delgado hitting the bar and Riggott clearing off the line.

Just past the mid-point of the second half, Pogatetz was involved in a sickening incident which looked bad at the time. We soon found out that a facial injury was to keep him out for the rest of the season.

After the game and phone-in, I bumped into Terry Butcher, former Ipswich and England captain and ex-manager in Scotland with Motherwell. He had been summarising for Channel 5. He's heading for Sydney and a job in the sun this summer.

We obviously chatted about the game, and Terry said, "What on earth was your manager doing? He was like the Grand Old Duke of York, up and down, up and down." Apparently McClaren had spent the match constantly switching seats between the directors box and dug-out. From where I had been sitting, I hadn't seen this, but I have to be honest and say I've seen it over the years. I believe it was something to do with Bill Beswick, the club's sports psychologist.

We boarded the bus and went straight back to the airport. The first person I bumped into was Gibbo. The two of us exchanged our frustrations at what we had witnessed and I took my usual seat at the back of the plane.

In flight, I went to do a Jimmy Riddle and, as I came out of the toilet, Stewart Downing's dad called me over for a chat with him and Stewart. We chatted for well over an hour about the game in general.

For me, there's not a better left-sided midfield player in the country than Stewart and I could never understand it when people were saying Kieran Richardson should have been in the England squad instead.

Downing has proved he can do it on the big stage. He produced the goods against Stuttgart, Roma and Basel. He gives the team shape, balance, pace, skill, creativity and goals. What a turnaround for a local lad who, two and half years ago, was destined for pastures new.

I personally believe McClaren would have offloaded him which would have been one of the biggest blunders of all-time. But, after his sensational month's loan at Sunderland, his talents were clearly highlighted. He returned and was handed a four-year contract. I wonder who sanctioned that?

When the plane landed at Durham Tees Valley Airport in the early hours of the morning the rain was bucketing down and the players and so-called VIPs had to queue in the elements with no shelter whatsoever.

But the saddest sight for me was seeing Pogatetz, hunched over, being wheeled over the tarmac with a blood-stained hanky covering his broken nose and cheek.

He looked a dejected figure, a terrible sight. Surely they could have had an ambulance on the runway to hide him away from probing eyes.

Eventually we arrive at passport control and I have to say those people are some of the weirdest characters I've set eyes on. No expression, deadpan and in need of a rocket up their arse. Do you know, the next time I'm going to grab one of them and see if I can feel a pulse. I don't think they're human, they may be robots.

Seriously though, I've noticed every time Yakubu goes through he's there for half-an-hour. Surely to God they know his background by now?

18. A stake through the heart of Dracula's boys

CUP

Alastair Brownlee

So Boro were in the semi-final and waiting for us were Steaua Bucharest. The first leg would be away from home and as the game in Romania would be followed just three days later by the FA Cup semi-final at Villa Park against West Ham, the return journey flight would drop the players at Birmingham airport before flying to Durham Tees Valley.

The implications of the itinerary became clear when I got a call from Bernie. "Al, is it true that we are not flying straight back?" It was a case of Xanthi all over again.

Everyone tried to help. This was, after all, a semi-final. Suggestions ranged from flying with the official party on the way out and coming straight back after the game with the fans, to getting off at Birmingham and Century hiring a car or getting on a train. Even Dave Allan sent a text asking him to be brave, as this was a massive game, but all to no avail.

I just sensed a growing unease in Bernie over the weekend and, on the Monday, he asked if I could arrange for someone to go in his place. A quick phone call later, Curtis Fleming was happy to step in.

Curtis even offered to let Bernie go if he changed his mind at the last minute, but the relief in Bernie's voice told the tale. Bernie would be in the studio and Curtis was going to Bucharest.

As we checked in, Curtis was in demand for interviews as he had played for Irish side Shelbourne against Steaua in the Champions League earlier in the season. The first leg in Ireland had been a creditable draw before Shelbourne had lost 4-1 in Romania. But Steaua had a couple of players sent off in that game, one of them the dangerous Dica, a sign perhaps that they could be temperamental.

Boro would be without Mark Viduka for the first leg as he had picked up a knock in the Easter Monday game with West Ham and remained behind getting treatment. This was a blow, as "The Duke" had hit top form in recent games and was sensational in the last round against Basel at the Riverside.

In the form he was in, he would be a cert for a World XI with his hold-up play and eye for goal, so he would be a big miss.

After a flight of just over three-and-a-half hours, the landing at Bucharest airport was sharp to say the least. The brakes were applied in dramatic fashion and there was an apology from the flight deck, "Sorry ladies and gentleman but there are workmen on the end of the runway and we had to pull up sharply." I shudder to think what Bernie's reaction would have been had he been on board!

Once we had collected our luggage, the importance of the game was clear as the tiny arrivals hall was crowded with TV crews and reporters all trying to get a word with the players. There were also some representatives of what seemed to be a lap-dancing bar - Club Max - handing out invitations. This promised to be an interesting trip!

Bucharest is quite clearly a city divided between the haves and the have-nots. We were staying in the JW Marriott Grand Hotel. And grand it certainly was, with a number of stylish restaurants, shopping mall with high quality goods, expensive cars parked outside and rooms that were the best I have stayed in.

Sadly, just out of the hotel, walk 100 yards and there are scenes of poverty, with children used as beggars for food or money. I found it a bit uncomfortable to see such a difference in lifestyles so close together.

Curtis said it had been worse when he was in Bucharest in 1989, just after the revolution that overthrew the country's former dictator Nicolae Ceausescu. He was playing for Dublin side, St Patrick's Athletic, who had been drawn against Dinamo Bucharest, and there were children without shoes on their feet roaming the streets like a scene out of *Oliver Twist*.

The game was to be held in the National Stadium, as Steaua's ground was undergoing redevelopment. There was only limited cover in a vast bowl of a stadium and fortunately it was above the press box, but as I sent the interview with Steve McClaren to Century, it was hard not to imagine the atmosphere the following day. With a full house anticipated, it was going to be a special 90 minutes.

Back at the hotel, we watched Arsenal defeat Villarreal 1-0 in the first leg of the Champions League semi final. The Spanish side had continued their progress after beating Boro in the UEFA cup group stage last season and you have to hope that one day we might also make it to the Champions League.

The following day, Boro's Academy boss Dave Parnaby and Eric Paylor joined Curtis and I for a look around the former dictator's palace. We somehow ended up in a deserted art gallery and, over coffee, chatted not about the exhibition but about the Academy and the impact that the young players had made this season.

Dave was naturally proud of the youngsters' achievements and remembered that in the match programme for the Basel game there was a photo showing the 19 England internationals the club had brought through at different levels, one of the products of the Academy - Matthew Bates - would pick up the Man of the Match award later on, but, as Dave mentioned, after they have done their work at the Academy it is then up to the manager to show faith in the youngsters and certainly Steve McClaren had been bold enough to give the kids their chance.

As we continued our long walk around the palace, we met a number of Boro fans all of whom said how friendly the locals had been. The Steaua fans had stressed that they did not fight, they just shouted loud. We were about to find that out.

The media bus set off in good time for the 8.45 local time kick-off. When we arrived at the stadium a good two hours before, it was already two-thirds full.

One familiar face walked to the press area. Fabrizio Ravanelli was a guest commentator for Italian television and I tried to get a chat with him, but he said he was too busy. Perhaps I should have sent Curtis to persuade him! The pair infamously had a training ground punch-up during their days together at Boro. So, the UEFA Cup campaign which began with Emerson at Xanthi, now saw Rav in Bucharest. Perhaps in Eindhoven, Juninho might turn up?

The atmosphere, as anticipated, was terrific. Even Chris Barnes, fitness coach, who always takes the team in the warm-up, was loudly booed as he put the cones down in the practice area. The home supporters were going to make this as intimidating as possible.

After a positive opening, all seemed under control until, from nowhere, Nicolae Dica hit an unstoppable shot into the top of the net after 30 minutes. As Curtis said in commentary, it was no use trying to blame anyone - sometimes you just have to say, 'Great goal', and it was.

After that, roared on by the majority of the 45,000 fans, Steaua turned up the heat. Schwarzer responded with three brilliant saves and Bates put in a top-drawer display in the absence of injured skipper, Southgate.

At the full-time whistle, it was still 1-0, the relief being the margin wasn't wider. As Steaua went on a Basel-style lap of honour, there were reasons for believing Boro were in the tie.

First of all, the lap of honour itself, as Mac said to the players, "Look at that and use it in the second leg. They think they are through." Secondly, Sorin Paraschiv and Banel Nicolita, both influential players, were booked and would miss the Riverside return, while Viduka would be fit for Boro.

Getting interviews after UEFA games is a bit of a scrum at the best of times. Tonight it would be a battle. A "mixed zone" – an area designated for media interviews – had been set up outside the main entrance, with at least a hundred journalists and cameramen all jostling for an interview with players as they made the short journey from the dressing rooms to team bus. The Romanians were on one side and we were on the other.

As soon as a player came out and stopped, there was a huge surge forward. Jimmy agreed to do an interview with me but, as soon as he started to speak he had to laugh, as about 50 microphones were thrust into his face. No wonder some players just keep their heads down and get on the bus. It's safer!

Back in the press box I sent the interviews back to Century and the local telecom engineer was still there refusing to leave until I was finished. As the Romanian currency couldn't be exchanged in the UK, I tried to give him a 'thank you', finding in my pocket a 150,000 Lei note. It sounds extravagant but it was the equivalent of about £2. At first, he refused and then, when I insisted, took the note.

He went away, coming back with his present for me... a packet of nuts. Now how do you explain a nut allergy? I decided not to, smiled, and gave the nuts to Curtis once my Romanian friend was out of sight.

It was after midnight when we got back to the hotel in time for a quick beer. With an FA Cup semi-final on Sunday and the return with Steaua only a week away the following seven days would test everyone to the limit.

Awaiting our flight back the manager did a chat about the West Ham game, but most of the journalists were concerned about the England job and the mounting speculation that Steve was about to be named as Sven's successor. But the manager played it all down.

I had an informal chat with Gareth about the tough run we were experiencing and the second leg. Gareth thought that 1-0 wasn't too bad a deficit to make up but that, against a side that conceded very few, the first goal at the Riverside would be crucial. I agreed, but how wrong we both would be.

The build-up to the Riverside second leg would have Boro bruised, both physically by West Ham's FA Cup tactics that left Mark Schwarzer with a cracked cheekbone, and mentally, by Marlon Harewood's late strike that put the Londoners in the final to face Liverpool.

So, it was down to the UEFA Cup to bring glory, and European football next season. But Steaua arrived in confident mood, their players believing they were just about through as they had a one-goal advantage, hadn't conceded an away goal so far, together with a terrific defensive record in their 12 games.

I went to the packed pre-match press conference at the Riverside, where Cosmin Olaroiu, the Steaua coach, was careful not to give too much away. But you could see he believed his side were favourites with his main concern, "Mark Viduka".

The game was a complete sell-out and, after the New Holgate End put on a great card display with the words EINDHOVEN 2006 spelled out in red and white, we were underway. For sheer football drama, this would even top the Basel game. It really was that good;

15 minutes – Despair. Dica scores after a scramble 0-1 aggregate 0-2

23 minutes – Dejection. Goian makes it 0-2, aggregate 0-3.

"And Boro's UEFA Cup hopes are collapsing around their ears."

33 minutes – Glimmer of hope, Maccarone hits a great shot 1-2, aggregate 1-3

At half-time the manager asks the team, "Do you believe you can score three goals in the second half?"

After a period of silence, Jimmy Floyd Hasselbaink stands up, "Yes, we bloody well can."

64 minutes – Growing belief. Mark Viduka heads in. 2-2, aggregate 2-3

78 minutes – Sheer bedlam "It's in, it's in, the Boro have scored, the Boro have scored and it's big Chris Riggott!"

Yes, Chris Riggott, who had missed a late chance in the FA Cup semi-final, had forced the ball in. It was now 3-2 to Boro on the night, 3-3 on aggregate.

Steaua were rocking. Mac's brave decision to put on four strikers, as he had deployed against Basel, was working a treat. Under sustained pressure on the pitch, together with a wall of sound generated by the fans, the Romanians were on the back foot.

Steaua were like a dazed boxer on the ropes, but could Boro land the knock-out blow?

With 60 seconds left, it was time for the 'boy wonder' to act.

Stewie Downing had produced a string of wonderful crosses all evening, but saved his best for last. His left foot sweetly swung the ball over. It was in that corridor of uncertainty between goalkeeper and defenders and made for an attacker to become a hero. And that hero was, unbelievably, Massimo Maccarone.

The ball flashed into the back of the net and the Riverside erupted.

"GOOOOOOAAAAAAALLLLLLL!!!! Massimo Maccarone has scored."

The press box reflected the jubilation as everyone leapt to their feet. Unfortunately, Bernie, in his emotion, hit me on the back of the head, sending my microphone soaring. The listeners heard a thump and probably thought I had passed out. Not true, but what a way it would have been to go! As I reeled in the microphone the celebrations continued.

"And Boro have struck a stake into the heart of Dracula's boys!"

But we still had stoppage time to play. Steaua's delaying tactics led to four minutes of time added on. If Maccarone hadn't scored we would have cheered the fourth official. As it was, it was bite-your-nails time.

Dica had a shot blocked by Ehiogu. Was it handball? "No" said the referee. Still time for a Steaua free-kick on the edge of the box. That was cleared and, at last, the whistle went... and

"It's Eindhoven, Eindhoven... we began in 1876, the infant Hercules, born out of the foundries of Teesside... mined out of the Eston Hills, is in the final of the UEFA Cup... party, party, party... everyone round my house for a parmo!"

As I have said earlier, you can't rehearse or prepare what you are going to say in moments like this. Who would have prepared for a 4-3 aggregate win over Steaua after being three-nil down?

I am a Boro lad, love the town and its history, together with a liking for our very own dish, and if any night deserved a parmo celebration it was this one.

The players were all ecstatic and went out on a lap of honour. This one was deserved as they had gone through to the final, but in the dressing room afterwards the champagne was unopened, as George Boateng said you only open champagne if you win something. We had achieved a great triumph but, as yet, had not secured the prize.

After the game, two comments had a tear rolling down the Brownlee microphone.

Gareth Southgate - "Ali is one of our biggest fans. I have asked him at the end of the season for a copy of the commentary on our UEFA Cup goals and I really look forward to hearing tonight's. He has been talking at the training ground all week about what this would mean and lifted the spirits after the FA Cup defeat. It's a great night."

Steve McClaren in the press conference - "Before the game we played a DVD of the Basel game, including Alastair Brownlee's commentary, to lift the players ahead of the game. It obviously worked."

Again, as in Rome, it really is a team effort on and off the pitch.

And so to home. Mrs B ran out of the house but forgot the step and fell into the garden, cutting her jeans... I think a liberal use of alcohol numbed the pain but, as she picked herself up, she came out with, "Did you know anything about a parmo party somewhere? The doorbell hasn't stopped ringing?"

The Linthorpe party, parmo or not, continued until the early hours.

It was still hard to take in the following day. What a match - and what a reaction. The e-mails flooded in to Century and a big "thank you" to everyone who kindly sent in their comments. For commercial radio, a rarity occurred, my commentary was played on the BBC in the Chris Moyles breakfast show on Radio 1 as a head-to-head with Paul Addison of Radio Cleveland and the parmo comment seemed to have struck a chord.

In the build-up to the final, Century produced parmo t-shirts and made a ringtone available with all the proceeds to charity, 21st Century Kids.

Joe Rigatoni's restaurant in Linthorpe Road also served up to Bernie and I the largest parmo in the world... not even I could get through the four-foot monster, so we served it up to the Boro fans outside the restaurant. It tasted good.

Boro were marching to the final with the parmo army!

Bernie Slaven

Two days before our game away to Portsmouth I discovered, while having a relaxing sauna with Ali at the Tall Trees, that there was a possibility that on the return flight we would be landing at Birmingham, then on to Teesside. The reason being the FA Cup semi-final clash against West Ham at Villa Park the following Sunday.

I totally understand the players are priority, but it's certainly no good for my welfare. On the Friday, I phoned Boro's PR man Dave Allan and asked him the question. He didn't know, but he assured me he would phone Graham Fordy and find out the answer.

Twenty-five minutes later, I received a text "Yes, landing in Birmingham, then onto Teesside. Bernie, be brave, you can't miss this one."

The following day, coming back from Portsmouth, I phoned Owen Ryan, whose our Century gaffer, and told him of my predicament. He said he would get back to me in the morning, and did as he promised. I told him outright that Ali's suggestion of me getting off in Birmingham and jumping on a train to Newcastle to do the Legends was outrageous.

1. It would highlight to everyone my phobia yet again. 2. It would mean travelling about 7-8 hours and it would be a total mess around.

Why not get some normal person to do the journey?

On Easter Monday, I arrived at the Riverside for a Premier League game with West Ham. Ali instantly said, "Well, Bernard?" He always calls me by my formal name when he's being serious. "What's going on then?"

I explained that I had phoned Owen and told him what I had said. Then, stupidly I suggested that I could go back with the fans. He said, "If that's possible I'm OK with that as long as we can get you there. You don't want to be missing this one, it's the semi-final, massive game."

Within half-an-hour, Ali's at me again.

"Bernard, why not just go with the official party?" I half-heartedly agreed that I would get sleeping tablets and go for it.

That night, just settling down to watch the highlights of the West Ham game on *Match of the Day*, I decided to text Ali.

"Al, no doubt Dave has had a word about the fans' flight back - no guarantees I wouldn't be sat with some loon. The more I think about Birmingham, the more I need whiskey, Valium and Prozac! The deal is, if you promise to try and get someone to replace me tomorrow and can't, I'll bite the bullet and promise you I'll go."

The return text read, "Slav UR2 good a mate 2 put you under any pressure and I won't do that. If, when I call 2morrow, u don't feel up to it that's fine."

The rest is history. I didn't make it to the game. I linked into the radio coverage before the game, at half-time and afterwards - from the safety of the Century studio in Gateshead.

Ali thought I didn't make the trip because of my fear of flying, but he was wrong.

The official party had received a letter from Graham Fordy saying don't wear jewellery. I couldn't get my ring off. A couple of nights before departing I watched the latest blockbuster movie, *Hostel*, where three lads go around Europe eventually arriving in, either Budapest or Bucharest. I'm not sure which it was, but I was taking no chances. They ended up getting taken hostage and were ripped apart by machete-wielding, saw-ripping maniacs. There was blood everywhere.

The game itself was disappointing. Defensively, we were sound for the opening 25 minutes, then bang - Dica hits a fantastic strike into the top left corner. Schwarzer had no chance. Just before half-time, Yakubu hit the bar from a Boateng cross and Morrison had a shot saved.

We were hemmed in for the majority of the second half and Schwarzer pulled off a couple of great saves. Steaua's Petre Marin missed a sitter late on and Massimo Maccarone had a 20-yard effort saved, but on the night we got what we deserved.

On the day of the second leg game, me and Ali must have spoken to each other about half a dozen times - the importance of the game was starting to tell.

We both arrived at the ground around five o'clock and performed our usual ritual of walking round the pitch, this time admiring the thousands of red and white cards which had been placed on the seats in the New Holgate.

They read "EINDHOVEN 2006" and were to provide a great display just before kick-off.

For the first time in a long time, the game was a sell-out. Neither of us could wait. At six I joined Malcolm and Eric on the Legends. Century FM had turned into Boro FM, as every caller was a Boro fan.

Eric decided to say, "If you're in a car on the way to the game with a group of mates, give us a call and sing us a Boro song." For the next two hours, every fan that came on sang their heart out. I was in absolute stitches with laughter.

I know at Middlesbrough we've not got a great deal of songs, but the one being sung on the airways was the best I'd heard for a while. We'd heard it before, now we were hearing it loud and clear, "Geordies at home, watching *The Bill*." It went on and on, and do you know what? I was loving every minute of it. Malcolm, at times, was interrupting asking, "Don't you know another line, good Lord?"

Nearing the end of the phone-in, Malcolm gave his prediction, "1-1 on the night, that means you'll be out." Eric said, "I reckon it will be a draw, but I sincerely hope you win." I tipped extra-time.

After 20 minutes, we found ourselves 2-0 down, 3-0 on aggregate. Southgate was off injured, the system we started with - three centre-backs and wing-backs - had to be dismantled and on came Massimo Maccarone.

We went 4-3-3 and looked better for it. Maccarone struck a fantastic shot across the keeper into the bottom corner. I personally looked at it as a consolation.

During the break I usually venture down to the press lounge, but I was so p***ed off I stayed at the back of the stand along with Dave Parnaby and my old team mate Gary Gill.

We were all shell-shocked. Dave looked as though he was going to break down. We all agreed that technically Steaua were far superior, quicker and that there was no way on earth we were going to come back - as I said, "Lightening doesn't strike twice."

Out came the players for the second half, and whatever had been said at half-time worked a treat.

The lads were like men possessed. Viduka added a second after a terrific ball from Downing, but we still had a mountain to climb.

With 18 minutes left, a Downing shot was parried into the path of Riggott and we were just one goal short. We had 18 minutes to score a goal to take us to dreamland.

In the final minute, Downing produced a magnificent cross from the left which Maccarone headed into the back of the net. As the ball went in, I jumped to my feet and had one of my mates hanging off my back. As I went to slap Ali on the back, he tilted his head and I knocked his microphone and earphones clean off!

Well, you should have seen his face. Despite the most crucial goal in our history he looked at me as if he was going to kill me.

He reclaimed his composure, and equipment, the final whistle went and the whole of Teesside was in disbelief. For the second time in three weeks we had come back from the dead, from three goals down, and we were now in the final of a major European competition.

Maccarone hit the headlines with his two goals, and rightly so. Hopefully those goals will have paid some of his £8m transfer fee back. Overall during his three-year stay, he's had an absolute nightmare, 93 games played and 21 goals scored, simply not good enough.

Half an hour after the game, a guy stood 40 yards away from me yelling "Tell the truth, Slaven!" I took my earphones off and said, "Who are you talking to? What is your problem?" Then I studied his face, and asked, "Aren't you the guy who was shouting 'you tosser' at me a couple of weeks back?"

"Yes, I was."

I said, "If you've got a problem with me, come and see me. You don't have to shout from 40 yards away. Right, what's your problem?"

He approached the press box before replying, "Well, I listen to you on the radio and you're forever saying 'Downing this and Downing that, he's a smashing player.' Well he's a coward, he doesn't tackle, he's no heart..."

He continued to rant. When he finished, I said, "I don't know if you're aware, but Downing set up three of the goals tonight?"

He replied, "I know, he was brilliant!" By now the guy was a lot closer, we'd finally agreed on something, I put my hand out and he shook it. Fantastic night.

On the way downstairs, I bumped into captain Gareth Southgate. I asked him how the injury was. "Hamstring pulled," was the reply. I wished him well and said I hoped he was back for the final.

As a former player, who was fortunate enough to play in a League Cup semi-final, ZDS cup final and be included in a World Cup squad - not forgetting an Autoglass Trophy and play-off final at Port Vale - my thoughts went out to players unfortunate not even to make the bench for Boro's UEFA Cup semi. The experienced Colin Cooper had missed out, as had young James Morrison, while Emanuel Pogatez and Gaizka Mendieta were both injured.

The following day I sent a text to Dave Allan asking if Keith Lamb would come on the Legends show, linking in by phone. Dave replied that he would see what he could so, but I heard nothing. When I arrived at Century, I was told Keith was coming in.

I thought it was a good idea to get him on after our achievement. Don't forget both Keith and Steve Gibson had come on the show when the flak was flying, so it was only right that they be invited on at such a high point, too.

Keith arrived late due to traffic problems. Back in my days as a player, he would have been fined! All the talk was obviously about the game.

Then I asked Keith, "Steve McClaren, what's the position with England?"

"Well, it's no secret Steve has spoken to the FA," replied Keith. "And we will not stand in his way if he wishes to go. It's a once-in-a-lifetime opportunity, every English manager's dream."

It seemed change was in the air as Boro prepared for the biggest game in the club's history.

19. Eindhoven May 10 2006

UEFA
CUP

Bernie Slaven

From the day we beat Bucharest, the town was absolutely buzzing. The Sevilla game couldn't come quickly enough. One day I picked up my son, Dominic, from school and, as soon as his backside hit the seat, he turned and said, "Dad, I want to go to Eindhoven with you."

"You can't come with me, I'm working," I replied. He had an answer. "Well, Mam can take me with Ryan."

I said, "Hold on a minute, you don't even go to the Riverside."

"So! I want to go to the final."

I explained that we were getting only 9,200 tickets and he finally accepted that he wouldn't be going, but I felt awful.

On the Friday before the game, Ali and I went to Joe Rigatoni's on Linthorpe Road to witness a monster parmo being made. The idea came from Ali's commentary when Maccarone scored Boro's fourth goal against Bucharest. Ali had ended his commentary with, "Everybody round my house for a parmo!"

This particular parmo was around four feet long and included 46 chicken breasts covered with cheese and breadcrumbs. It was absolutely massive and took six people to carry it. After posing for photographs for the *Evening Gazette* and *Northern Echo* and holding interviews with Tyne Tees and Sky, we distributed the parmo to passers by. It went within 20 minutes and now I know why Ali resembles a spacehopper – fat and round with a big pair of ears!

Leaving Rigatoni's we headed for Bakers Tailoring, a stone's throw away. When we arrived, Adil Ditta, the owner, said, "Lads, you know we've made the suits which the team are going to wear in the final? Well, I would like to dress you two up as well." What a gesture.

We ended up with a quality suit each, shirt shoes and red tie which the players would be wearing in Eindhoven. Ali's suit was more expensive than mine for obvious reasons – the tailor needed a greater amount of material.

The biggest talking point leading up to the final was obviously Steve McClaren being named England manager. I personally couldn't see the benefit of announcing it a week before the final.

On the Legends, we were inundated with texts referring to Steve's appointment and one of the funniest ones read, "What on earth's going on with England? When it comes to appointing managers, we have had a turnip, a Swede and now a carrot head."

I picked Ali up at seven in the morning on the day we set off. Durham Tees Valley Airport resembled Heathrow. It was jam-packed. We left a special atmosphere behind and headed for Holland.

Our media bus was waiting for us at Eindhoven, but some members of the travelling party were less then impressed when we landed at our accommodation. This time we were not staying in a hotel, rather a Center Parcs complex about half-an-hour outside the city. We were in the middle of woodland surrounded by wild boar, bears and beaver!

Before arriving at our new abode, we went to PSV's stadium for the pre-match press conference, where we heard from Steve McClaren, Stuart Parnaby and Chris Riggott, who all faced the world's media. The two young lads didn't look comfortable. I would like to know why the manager picked these guys and not a Southgate, Viduka or Hasselbaink - experienced campaigners.

To the left of the top table was, unguarded, the UEFA Cup. Ali and I could not resist going up and posing for pictures alongside it.

After the session, we headed back to the jungle, had a quick wash then returned to PSV's stadium to check the gear worked and to join Eric and Malcolm on the Legends. As expected, the show was populated with excited Boro fans. Afterwards we headed for something to eat, then bed. No late night this time.

The following morning, we headed to the city centre after breakfast. It was heaving with both sets of supporters thoroughly enjoying the occasion, mixing, mingling and exchanging scarves, flags and hats. The sunshine was glorious and this was a perfect setting.

After posing for hundreds of pictures with the travelling red army we went to Sky presenter David Craig's hotel to change into our flash suits - no need to return to the woodland.

Just before we jumped into a taxi and headed for the ground, the hotel porter came up and asked if I was from the pop band, Il Divo, the Italian operatic singers. I replied, "No, we're better. The only similarity is one of them has got a quiff like mine!"

The build-up to the game was fantastic. Sevilla fans were in the ground two hours before kick-off, singing their hearts out. Only half of Boro's support were in early, the other half still in the pubs, no doubt. It's the British mentality, I suppose, but you would have thought they would have given a couple of pints up to get to the final earlier.

Just before kick-off, a host of children along with gymnasts put on a superb display which ended when they released large orange balloons.

There was speculation the night before the game that Ray Parlour was going to play right side. I'd mentioned it on the Legends and the fans were up in arms about it.

But Ray was on the bench and James Morrison, who I was hoping would play, started. I thought the formation, 4-4-2, was good enough and the team was definitely right.

We looked nervy in the opening part of the game, whereas Sevilla stroked the ball about and were accurate with their passing. They were lightening quick, and over the course of the 90 minutes, proved they were ruthless.

Their opening goal was a fine header, but Fabio Rochemback, who I thought started well, didn't close down and Luis Fabiano nipped in behind Riggott and headed past Mark Schwarzer, who had no chance.

After the break, McClaren tried to change things and brought on Massimo Maccarone. To be fair, he perked things up. Viduka had a golden opportunity when he latched on to a cushioned header from Riggott. I was hoping he was going to play the ball with the inside of his foot and put the ball into the corner, but he went for power and gave the goalkeeper an opportunity. A quarter of an hour later, Viduka was set up by Hasselbaink, but shot wide.

Sometimes in football you just have to hold your hands up and say you were beaten by the better side. Sevilla were outstanding on the night, they proved they are a quality side.

They had five pacey guys who I couldn't have caught in a car. They were lightning quick and, in the end, contributed greatly to a record. I beleive it was the first time in 21 years a team had been beaten by four in a UEFA Cup final.

Getting beaten by one would have been hard to take, but getting walloped by four turned it into a nightmare.

We did what we had to after the game. We'd been on air from six and it was now 11, but we'd had enough and knew how the fans felt.

The mood on the way back to where we were staying was sombre. What do you expect? It remained sombre the next morning. There wasn't much conversation on the delayed flight back to Teesside.

Alastair Brownlee

Saturday May 6 saw the UEFA Cup Final media day at the Riverside. As I arrived, a lot of clearly upset fans were at main entrance. They were unfortunate not to have received a ticket for the final. It was heartbreaking to hear their personal stories but what can you do when a relatively small stadium hosts a major final and the club receives only 9,200 tickets?

Perhaps in future UEFA should only select grounds with a 50,000-plus capacity. After all, in Holland the Amsterdam Arena would have coped with demand but that was little consolation to the distraught fans.

The only slight criticism I have is that since the UEFA Cup journey began in 2004, only 32 fans had attended every tie. Surely, as a PR exercise, the 32 should have received their tickets first and have been made part of the official party. Instead, I know personally of two from the 32 who eventually got seats but had to sweat until the Monday before the final. It shouldn't have come to that.

The media day also gave a chance to say congratulations to Steve McClaren on getting the England job. Steve undoubtedly left Boro in a stronger shape than when he arrived. He is a fiercely ambitious individual and I have enjoyed working with him.

A Robbo, he isn't. He didn't let the local media establish the same close rapport, but he knows exactly what he wants to achieve in football and he is clearly on target.

I thank him for all he has done for Boro, wish I had got to know him personally a bit better, but share his taste in music. He asked me on an away trip for two Chris Rea tickets for him and his son and, thanks to Owen Ryan at Century, I was able to come up with the goods. It's a fool who thinks it's over for Steve. He has hit the top job in England and I wish him all the best.

As the clock slowly ticked down towards the final, the whole town of Middlesbrough seemed to be dressed in red and white. I spent a morning with Karen Shields from Middlesbrough Town Centre Company judging shop window displays, tried to find the space in the stomach to eat the four-foot parmo, or at least part of it, while Bernie and I were dressed for the final by Adil Ditta, the owner of Bakers Tailoring, with the present of new suits together with the same red tie that the players had chosen to go with their matchday suits. The build up was going well.

Just before going home to pack, I joined Colin Cooper in Captain Cook Square to release over 4,000 red and white balloons. Colin was superb, as he stayed for over an hour making sure that everyone who wanted an autograph received one and was, as always, a great ambassador for the club.

Just 24 hours earlier, Colin had played his final game for Boro, coming on as substitute in a 1-0 defeat at Fulham. It was a team that had at one stage 11 graduates from the Academy on the pitch, setting a Premiership record. But a sign of the respect the youngsters have for Colin was made as soon as he stepped on the field when Lee Cattermole gave him the captain's armband.

Lee had set a record in the same game by becoming Boro's youngest ever skipper, but it was a great gesture to hand the role over to Coops, who ended his playing days as Boro's oldest captain, 20 years and 400 appearances after making his league debut for the club.

A Middlesbrough Football Club without Colin seems unthinkable and, as he progresses towards his UEFA A licence, he will still be part of the fabric at the training ground, helping the many talented young players coming from the Academy.

It was a pity that Coops hadn't been at least on the bench when Boro won the Carling Cup that started the whole Euro adventure, but he didn't sulk at Steve McClaren's decision in Cardiff and cheered the team on from the stands.

Again, he would miss out on a UEFA Cup final place, but once more he would be cheering the team on with the 9,000 fans who had tickets and the many more who would travel to Eindhoven in the hope of getting in.

Tuesday May 9 and Bernie picked me up just after seven as we set off for the airport. Stuart Boyd would also be on the trip as our touchline reporter. Durham Tees Valley Airport was heaving with fans looking forward to the big day. Many were wearing the parmo cup final t-shirts that Century had produced and had mobiles with the ringtone of my slightly over-the-top commentary on the semi-final. In total, over £20,000 was raised from t-shirts and ringtones, with the proceeds going to 21st Century Kids, helping disadvantaged youngsters in the north east.

After a smooth flight, we landed in Eindhoven in sweltering temperatures and headed for the Philips Stadion, the home of PSV, where Steve McClaren, Chris Riggott and Stuart Parnaby would attend a press conference.

As we headed for the media bus, booming out around the car park was the Brownlee ringtone. The culprit was Gary Thorburn, who had found from somewhere a megaphone, much to the amusement of arriving passengers who were serenaded by invites round to my house for a parmo!

The UEFA press conference made you realise what a big stage Boro had arrived on. The room was packed with reporters, photographers and TV crews from around the world, with the only slight problem being that Steve McClaren's earpiece, providing a translation from Spanish to English, failed to work as the manager was asked the same question four times. All he could do was shrug his shoulders. Eventually one of journalists had sympathy and provided a translation.

Our accommodation was about 20 minutes from Eindhoven in a Center Parcs complex. David Craig, Sky Sports, found the situation totally unsuitable as he had to do regular updates from around the city squares and this would have meant constant taxi journeys backwards and forwards.

So Sky booked David into the Sofitel in Eindhoven, the only problem being a huge demand for accommodation had driven room prices through the roof. The cost was 700 euros per night!

It was a bit strange preparing for the final in a lodge in the middle of the woods alongside families on holiday, and a few members of the media complained that it was difficult to get into working mode as the ice-cream flowed, but it was a small price to pay for experiencing a major cup final.

We went back to the stadium to watch Boro's final training session, Bernie came along as the lodges didn't have telephones. I was going to try and sort something out so that he could join in the Legends. Either that or he would have to go back and sit amongst the wildlife.

The home of PSV was not much larger than the Riverside and, as the players went through their paces, they should, I thought, feel at ease, unlike Bernie who was asked to leave the press box with the rest of the media after the first 15 minutes of training, cutting his participation in the Legends short!

After much pleading with various officials and a payment of 400 euros, an isdn line – a high-speed telephone line - was placed in the media room and Bernie was back on air, but it was turning into an expensive trip!

Cup final day dawned with clear blue skies and nerves in the stomach. We arrived outside the ground by midday and went in search of David Craig's hotel. David had kindly let us use his room so as to avoid going back to the woods later on.

The squares were filling up with Sevilla and Boro fans, all mixing well. Worryingly, the support from Spain was very, very confident.

Whilst Bernie topped up his tan and signed endless autographs, I headed back to the ground, ITV had asked me to do an interview with newsman Tim Rogers into the main news at one to explain to the rest of the country what a parmo was. This was getting a bit out of hand!

Afterwards, Simon O'Rourke from Tyne Tees grabbed me for a chat about the game. But, just as he asked the first question, the PA system burst into life, drowning everything out as they started a rehearsal for the pre-match entertainment.

It was a real *It'll be Alright on the Night* moment and a good job that, as Teesside knows, I have a loud voice!

I caught up with Bernie and all of Teesside seemed to be in Eindhoven. He and I went to the hotel to get changed into those cup final suits.

At first we had a problem getting in, as Mr Slaven, unshaven and wearing a T-shirt and scruffy jeans, was frowned upon by the doorman who couldn't believe that Bernard was staying in such a high-class establishment so refused admission. As the Boro legend's blood pressure soared, I finally persuaded the reluctant doorman to let him in, but only after producing the room key.

Thirty minutes later, as a freshly shaven and new-suited Slaven walked out of the hotel, the doorman took a second look only to get a, "Up your kilt!" Bernard doesn't forgive easily.

It promised to be a long stint behind the microphone as we were to present the news at 5.30, pre-match phone in from six and then seven until 11 match commentary and post-match calls. Bernie and Stuart can both access the loo but, as I am on air most of the time, I have to exercise a certain amount of bladder control!

The build up to the game was fantastic, with a great show on the pitch by local schoolchildren and artists, the type of entertainment you watch on TV before any major sporting event. But I was watching this all unfold before Boro would participate in the final. You really had to pinch yourself.

Once all the pre -match formalities had been observed, the real business began, and it started with Boro defending the end of the ground that housed the majority of their support in what was Steve McClaren's 250th and final game as manager of Middlesbrough Football Club.

Quite clearly, Sevilla were a top-class side and caused us plenty of problems before Luis Fabiano's header clipped the inside of the post and went into the net, giving them the lead after 27 minutes.

McClaren swopped Maccarone for Morrison at half-time and Mark Viduka failed to convert a great chance from a Chris Riggott knockdown. I looked at Bernie, who felt the striker should have placed it and not gone for power, but the chance was gone.

Twenty minutes left and a limping Franck Queudrue made way for Yakubu. We had four forwards on the pitch as the comeback kings of Europe went for it again. Sadly, this time it was not to be. However, the referee, Herbert Fandel from Germany, failed to spot a clear foul on Viduka in the penalty area. That was a key moment, as seconds later, the game was over with Enzo Maresca's shot making it 2-0.

Maresca and Freddie Kanoute added further goals in the last ten minutes. Sevilla deserved their win, they were the better side, but what might have happened had the referee given the spot kick? Sadly, we will never know...

As we found out at Wembley in the Zenith Data Systems Cup, League Cup and FA Cup finals, losing is a bitter pill to swallow. The players collected their runners-up medals and thanked the fans before heading to the dressing room. Sevilla players and fans partied. We would have done the same.

This was now the toughest part of the entire trip as we still had a full hour's phone-in to complete when all we wanted to do was pack up the equipment and go home.

Stuart Boyd brought back an interview with Steve Gibson. The chairman had gone into the dressing room after Steve McClaren had thanked the players for all their efforts to reassure the players that the future was bright and, despite the manager leaving a new appointment wouldn't break the foundations that had been put in place.

It was typical of Steve Gibson. He rarely goes into the dressing room, but sensing that this was a critical moment, the chairman provided the inspiration to lift broken hearts and boost the players' spirits.

Eventually the media bus set off back to Center Parcs. It was a quiet journey and, after finishing what had been a demanding schedule, like most Boro fans I shed a few tears. We had been so close.

The journey back to Teesside couldn't come quickly enough and, as we left the departure lounge at Eindhoven airport some Sevilla fans were also going home. But they were clearly still in party mood. Not for the last time I thought. "That could have been us."

After arriving home, Tyne Tees called to ask if I could have a chat into their six o'clock programme from the Riverside. It was probably the last place I wanted to be, as this would have been the destination for the victory parade.

But I went along and, as reporter Greg Eastell mentioned, the barriers had been put in place in preparation for the parade but instead the car park was deserted.

It will take time for the wounds of Eindhoven to heal, but I hope this book is a reminder of just what an amazing journey it was for the small town in Europe to make the final and that achievement should be praised.

On the Sunday after the final, I attended the Teesside Junior Football Alliance cup finals day at Rockliffe Park. Hundreds of youngsters all enjoyed their big day and it was a lift to the spirits after the UEFA Cup final.

As I waited to hand out the trophies, Chris Ord, Secretary of the TJFA, said, "Everyone should be proud to be here. To get to a final of any competition takes a great team effort and, although there is disappointment if things didn't go your way today, on a cup final day we don't use the word losers. There are only winners and runners-up. To make a final is a massive achievement and that should be recognised."

The sentiments fitted the professional world just as well as the young hopefuls.

Middlesbrough Football Club, UEFA Cup Runners-Up 2006.

20. Reflections

UEFA CUP

Bernie Slaven

The two years on the road to Eindhoven have been an absolute dream.

I was brought up on European football in Glasgow, but I've been here on Teesside 20 years now and, until recently I've never been anywhere near it - I didn't even play in the Anglo-Italian Cup!

This has been a dream come true. In our first season in the competition we got to the last 16, which was a good achievement. In our second year, we get to the final.

We've played some quality sides and some pub teams along the way. Ostrava, Xanthi and Egaleo, personally I'd never heard of these teams. Even when we played Lazio, I thought they were like Coventry on the night.

But then we played some serious opposition. Stuttgart were a quality side. Basel, with the two goals on their own patch, showed they were a good side. Bucharest technically were better than us, but we had more fire in our bellies in the return leg.

Getting to the final was an outstanding achievement from everyone. The players and management alike, and obviously I'm delighted for Steve Gibson.

20. Steve McClaren

Bernie Slaven

I can recall when Steve got the job at Middlesbrough. He asked to see me at Hurworth. When I arrived at the training ground, he came sauntering down the stairs.

He was wearing his trademark smile and thanked me for going along for a chat. I joked, "Have you asked me up because you want to sign me, or have you asked me because you want to pick my brains?" It was obviously the latter.

We went to his office and had a good chat for 40 minutes. He asked me things about the team, the players, the problems. I replied that too many players had been played out of position and that too many players were too close to the previous manager, Bryan Robson, socially.

I told him that, regarding my radio and TV duties I was honest and outspoken. He said, "That's your job, no doubt we'll have tiffs along the way." I left the training ground thinking, "This guy is no mug, he's finding out exactly what he's coming into."

Everyone in life has plusses and minuses. Steve was ultra professional. During his five-year reign, I didn't read one bit of bad press regarding any of his players. That's to his credit, unlike our north east rivals, who are scarcely out of the press. He brought the club its first-ever trophy when winning the Carling Cup, two FA Cup semi-finals, a UEFA Cup final and our highest-ever Premier League position.

Despite the success over five years, Steve never became a firm favourite with the fans. In my humble opinion, saying in press conferences we were magnificent when clearly we were far from it didn't wash with the public. In fact, it was an insult to their intelligence. It was spin and kidology. Then he was quoted as saying entertainment didn't matter. Well, if Steve was paying £500 for a season ticket I'm sure he would have been demanding more.

Then, to inflame his relationship with the supporters, he said they needed educating. Jose Mourinho had said that at Chelsea and got away with it. Unfortunately, Steve couldn't.

My own relationship with him never blossomed after the first couple of years. Whenever we met he would have a shake of the hand and a quick chat. I remember one day he said, "If you want to know more, phone me." I never took him up on that.

During the last couple of years of his reign we didn't acknowledge each other much. No doubt he had heard stories about what had been said on the Legends show, or what I had said. Whatever I said to offend, annoy, or bug him was not intentional. It was my professional opinion for which I'm paid. There was no malice, vindictiveness or backstabbing on my part.

On Thursday May 4 Steve was named England manager. It was the worst secret in football. Scolari was supposedly number one choice. I didn't believe it. I sincerely wish Steve and his family all the very best in the future and hope he has great success with England. At least for my sons' sake! And I would like to thank him for bringing major success to the team that I played for and that I now support.

Letter to Boro chairman Steve Gibson

You have the satisfaction of knowing that, although your team did not win the game, your supporters present in Eindhoven proved to the world that football fans can turn a match into a friendly, violence-free celebration.

In this respect, we were most impressed with your supporters, who displayed great sportsmanship in acknowledging and accepting the final result.

We would like to compliment you on the remarkable campaign conducted by Middlesbrough FC on the way to the first UEFA Cup final in the club's history, as well as the manner in which your players, despite their disappointment, accepted the verdict of their defeat to Sevilla.

Unfortunately, every final decides one winner and one loser. Nevertheless, your club's achievement in reaching the final reflects the professional attitude and commitment of your team and of the club's officials, and confirms that Middlesbrough FC is a proud member of the European football elite.

We should also like to express our sincere gratitude to you, every one of your club's officials and staff, for the competent and friendly co-operation they offered us at all times this season, both at your home matches at the Riverside Stadium as well as during the final in Eindhoven.

Lars-Christer Olsson
Chief executive of UEFA

Match Facts

Thursday September 16 2004

Venue: Riverside Stadium
Result: **Middlesbrough 3 Banik Ostrava 0**
Goalscorers: Hasselbaink 56, Viduka 62, 80
Teams
Middlesbrough: Schwarzer; Parnaby, Riggott, Southgate (Capt.), Queudrue, Nemeth, Parlour, Boateng, Zenden, Viduka, Hasselbaink. Unused subs: Nash (gk); Cooper, McMahon, Doriva, Downing, Morrison, Job.
Banik Ostrava: Raska; Latal (Capt.), Drozd, Bystron, Cizek, Besta, Pospech, Dvornik (Velkoborsky 15), Zebek, Matusovic (Papadopulos 87), Licka (Lukes 65). Unused subs: Konig (gk); Zavadil, Hoffman, Zurek.
Referee: Pascal Garibian, France.
Bookings
Middlesbrough: Parlour 43, foul on Matusovic.
Banik Ostrava: Velkoborsky 36, foul on Zenden.
Attendance: 29,746
Conditions: Slight breeze, quite warm.

Thursday September 30 2004

Venue: Bazaly Stadium
Result: **Banik Ostrava 1 Middlesbrough 1**
Goalscorers: Bystron 19, Morrison 90
Teams
Banik Ostrava: Raska; Latal (Capt.), Bystron, Cizek, Besta, Pospech, Dvornik, Zubek (Zurek 68), Matusovic, Papadopulos (Velkoborsky 80), Licka. Unused subs: Bucek (gk); Drozd, Kotrys, Hoffman, Varadi.
Middlesbrough: Schwarzer; Parnaby, Southgate (Capt.), Cooper, Queudrue, Morrison, Boateng, Doriva, Downing, Zenden, Nemeth (Christie 82). Unused subs: Nash (gk); McMahon, Bates, Wheater, Taylor, Mendieta.
Referee: Matteo Tresoloni, Italy.
Sent-off: Queudrue 58, booked for foul on Matusovic after being booked for deliberate handball after 48 minutes.
Bookings
Banik Ostrava: Papadopulos 3, deliberate handball.
Middlesbrough: None
Attendance: 15,351
Conditions: Cool, still and dry.

Thursday October 21 2004

Venue:	Georgios Kamaras Stadium
Result:	**Egaleo 0 Middlesbrough 1**
Goalscorer:	Downing 77
Teams	
Egaleo:	Sidibe; Papoutsis, Alexopoulos, Psomas, Edusei, Fotakis, Skopelitis, Barkoglou (Christou 90), Chloros, Nikolopoulos (Makris 76), Manousakis. Unused subs: Klajevic (gk); Liapakis, Tsatos, Chatzis, Tsagavelis.
Middlesbrough:	Schwarzer; McMahon, Riggott, Southgate (Capt.), Cooper, Morrison (Mendieta 46), Parlour, Doriva, Zenden (Downing 69), Nemeth, Viduka (Hasselbaink 69). Unused subs: Nash (gk); Ehiogu, Boateng, Wilson.
Referee:	Attila Hanacsek, Hungary.
Bookings	
Egaleo:	Alexopoulos 89, foul on Mendieta.
Middlesbrough:	McMahon 27, foul on Edusei; Morrison 43, foul on Alexopoulos.
Attendance:	2,689
Conditions:	Warm and sticky, no wind.

Thursday November 4 2004

Venue:	Riverside Stadium
Result:	**Middlesbrough 2 Lazio 0**
Goalscorer:	Zenden 16, 71
Teams	
Middlesbrough:	Schwarzer; McMahon, Riggott, Southgate (Capt.), Queudrue, Parlour, Boateng, Zenden, Downing, Viduka, Hasselbaink (Job 81). Unused subs: Nash (gk); Cooper, Doriva, Morrison, Wilson, Davies.
Lazio:	Casazza; Couto, Lopez, Oddo, Seric; Dabo, Giannichedda (Melara 13), Filippini. Di Canio, Cesar, Delgado (Rocchi 50). Unused subs: De Angelis (gk); Manfredini, Pandev, Sannibale, Torroni.
Referee:	Mr Yuri Baskakov, Russia.
Bookings	
Middlesbrough:	None.
Lazio:	None.
Attendance:	33,991
Conditions:	Cool and still

...ining in the Philips Stadion

Mark Schwarzer was to play in the final wearing a protective mask after breaking a cheekbone in the FA Cup semi-final against West Ham three weeks earlier

Alastair and Bernie outside the ground where the 2006 UEFA Cup final would be played

Left to right - Alastair, Boro chief executive Keith Lamb, Bernie, Boro chairman Steve Gibson in Eindl

ow if these two HAD been in charge it would have been 8!

Boro fans in Eindhoven

More Boro fans in Eindhoven

*Alastair and Bernie in the
press box in the PSV Stadium*

ide the PSV Stadium

a with their own display at the back of an on-field pre-match display

Franck Queudrue

Lee Cattermole has come a long way since his first team debut at Newcastle on Jan 2 2006

dejected bunch

No need to add anything

Full Time Report
Final - Wednesday 10 May 2006
PSV Stadion - Eindhoven

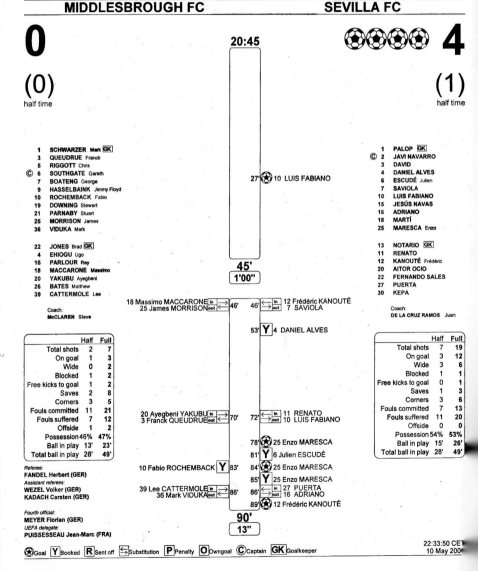

MIDDLESBROUGH FC   SEVILLA FC

0   20:45   ⚽⚽⚽⚽ **4**

(0)   **(1)**
half time   half time

Middlesbrough FC		Sevilla FC	
1	SCHWARZER Mark GK	1	PALOP GK
3	QUEUDRUE Franck	© 2	JAVI NAVARRO
5	RIGGOTT Chris	3	DAVID
© 6	SOUTHGATE Gareth	4	DANIEL ALVES
7	BOATENG George	6	ESCUDÉ Julien
9	HASSELBAINK Jimmy Floyd	7	SAVIOLA
10	ROCHEMBACK Fabio	10	LUIS FABIANO
19	DOWNING Stewart	15	JESÚS NAVAS
21	PARNABY Stuart	16	ADRIANO
25	MORRISON James	18	MARTÍ
36	VIDUKA Mark	25	MARESCA Enzo
22	JONES Brad GK	13	NOTARIO GK
4	EHIOGU Ugo	11	RENATO
15	PARLOUR Ray	12	KANOUTÉ Frédéric
18	MACCARONE Massimo	20	AITOR OCIO
20	YAKUBU Ayegbeni	22	FERNANDO SALES
26	BATES Matthew	27	PUERTA
39	CATTERMOLE Lee	30	KEPA

Coach:
McCLAREN Steve

Coach:
DE LA CRUZ RAMOS Juan

27' ⚽ 10 LUIS FABIANO

45'
1'00"

18 Massimo MACCARONE [in] → | 46'   46' | ← [in] 12 Frédéric KANOUTÉ
25 James MORRISON [out] ← | | [out] → 7 SAVIOLA

53' **Y** 4 DANIEL ALVES

	Half	Full
Total shots	2	7
On goal	1	3
Wide	0	2
Blocked	1	2
Free kicks to goal	1	2
Saves	2	8
Corners	3	5
Fouls committed	11	21
Fouls suffered	7	12
Offside	1	2
Possession	46%	47%
Ball in play	13'	23'
Total ball in play	28'	49'

	Half	Full
Total shots	7	19
On goal	3	12
Wide	3	6
Blocked	1	1
Free kicks to goal	0	1
Saves	1	3
Corners	3	6
Fouls committed	7	13
Fouls suffered	11	20
Offside	0	0
Possession	54%	53%
Ball in play	15'	26'
Total ball in play	28'	49'

20 Ayegbeni YAKUBU [in] → | 70'   72' | ← [in] 11 RENATO
3 Franck QUEUDRUE [out] ← | | [out] → 10 LUIS FABIANO

78' ⚽ 25 Enzo MARESCA
81' **Y** 6 Julien ESCUDÉ

10 Fabio ROCHEMBACK **Y** 83'   84' ⚽ 25 Enzo MARESCA

85' **Y** 25 Enzo MARESCA

39 Lee CATTERMOLE [in] → | 86'   86' | ← [in] 27 PUERTA
36 Mark VIDUKA [out] ← | | [out] → 16 ADRIANO

89' ⚽ 12 Frédéric KANOUTÉ

90'
13"

Referee:
FANDEL Herbert (GER)
Assistant referees:
WEZEL Volker (GER)
KADACH Carsten (GER)

Fourth official:
MEYER Florian (GER)
UEFA delegate:
PUISSESSEAU Jean-Marc (FRA)

22:33:50 CET
10 May 2006

⚽ Goal   **Y** Booked   **R** Sent off   ⇄ Substitution   **P** Penalty   **O** Owngoal   © Captain   **GK** Goalkeeper

UEFA's match facts from the final

Thursday November 25 2004

Venue:	El Madrigal Stadium
Result:	**Villarreal 2 Middlesbrough 0**
Goalscorers:	Guayre 37, Javi Venta 74

Teams

Villarreal: Reina; Gonzalo, Arruabarrena, Quique Alvarez (Capt), Javi Venta, S. Cazorla, Josico, Guayre (Xisco Nadal 86), Arzo, Riquelme (Armando Sa 86), Font. Unused subs: Lopez Vallejo (gk); Pena, Jonathan, Marcos.

Middlesbrough: Schwarzer; McMahon (Reiziger 72), Riggott, Southgate (Capt.), Queudrue, Doriva (Hasselbaink 46), Nemeth, Boateng, Zenden, Downing, Job (Viduka 46). Unused subs: Nash (gk); Cooper, Parlour, Morrison.

Referee: Jan Wegerees, Holland.

Bookings

Villarreal: None.

Middlesbrough: Southgate 31, foul on Riquelme; Zenden 81, foul on Arzo.

Attendance: 14,250

Conditions: Pleasantly warm and still

Wednesday December 15 2004

Venue:	Riverside Stadium
Result:	**Middlesbrough 3 Partizan Belgrade 0**
Goalscorers:	Nemeth 9, Job 22, Morrison 90.

Teams

Middlesbrough: Schwarzer; Reiziger, Cooper, Southgate (Capt.), Queudrue, Doriva, Parlour (Morrison 64), Zenden, Downing, Job, Nemeth. Unused subs: Nash (gk); Davies, McMahon, Hasselbaink, Viduka, Wilson.

Partizan Belgrade: Kralj (Pantic 40); Mirkovic, Brnovic, Boya, Ciric (Vukcevic 46), Djordjevic, Emeghara, Tomic, Ilic (Capt.) (Grubjesic 71), Rnic, Nadj (Capt from 71). Unused subs: Bajic, Radovic, Petrovic, Babovic.

Referee: Grzegorz Gilewski. Poland.

Bookings

Middlesbrough: Parlour 5, foul on Nadj; Queudrue 63, foul on Boya

Partizan Belgrade: Boya 11, foul on Cooper.

Attendance: 20,856

Conditions: Cool and still

Thursday February 17 2005

Venue:	Arnold Schwarzenegger Stadium
Result:	**Grazer AK 2 Middlesbrough 2**
Goalscorers:	Zenden 52, Bazina 64, Hasselbaink 65, Kollmann 79.
Teams	
Grazer AK:	Schranz; Tokic, Ehmann, Muratovic, Pogatetz, Bleidelis (Standfest 70), Dollinger (Amerhauser 72), Aufhauser (Sick 90), Bazina, Plassnegger, Kollmann. Unused subs: Almer (gk); Ramusch, Skoro, Majstorovic.
Middlesbrough:	Schwarzer; Reiziger, Riggott, Southgate, Queudrue, Morrison, Doriva, Parlour, Zenden, Downing, Hasselbaink. Unused subs: Nash (gk); Parnaby, Cooper, Davies, Nemeth, Job, Graham.
Referee:	Edo Trivkovic, Croatia.
Sent-off:	Kollmann, yellow card 23, dissent and 80 diving.
Bookings	
Grazer AK:	None.
Middlesbrough:	Reiziger 52, foul on Dollinger; Riggott 57, time wasting; Southgate 85, foul on Muratovic; Hasselbaink 90, dissent.
Attendance:	13,000
Conditions:	Approaching freezing, dry. (But warmer than Bolton the previous Saturday!)

Thursday February 24 2005

Venue:	Riverside Stadium
Result:	**Middlesbrough 2 Grazer AK 1**
Goalscorers:	Bazina 8, Morrison 18, Hasselbaink 61.
Teams	
Middlesbrough:	Schwarzer; Reiziger, Riggott, Southgate, Queudrue, Morrison (Parnaby 46), Parlour, Zenden, Downing (Nemeth 86), Job (Doriva 46), Hasselbaink. Unused subs: Nash (gk); Cooper, Davies, Graham.
Grazer AK:	Schranz; Tokic, Ehmann, Muratovic, Pogatetz, Bleidelis (Standfest 64), Majstorovic (Dollinger 74), Aufhauser, Bazina, Plassnegger, Skoro. Unused subs: Almer (gk); Ramusch, Amerhauser, Six, Sick.
Referee:	Eduardo Gonzalez, Spain.
Bookings	
Middlesbrough:	Doriva 82, persistent misconduct.
Grazer AK:	Bazina 8, ungentlemanly conduct; Amerhauser 23, foul on Parlour; Ehmann 69, foul on Downing.
Attendance:	20,371
Conditions:	Cold, windy, occasional drizzle and hail.

Thursday March 10 2005

Venue: Riverside Stadium
Result: **Middlesbrough 2 Sporting Lisbon 3**
Goalscorers: Pedro Barbosa 48, Liedson 52, Douala 64, Job 79, Riggott 86.
Teams
Middlesbrough: Schwarzer; Reiziger (Nemeth 46), Riggott, Southgate, Queudrue, Parnaby, Doriva, Zenden, Downing, Hasselbaink, Graham (Job 52). Unused subs: Jones (gk); McMahon, Cooper, Wheater, Johnson.
Sporting Lisbon: Ricardo; Hugo, Barbosa (Capt.) (Sa Pinto 77), Enakarhire, Douala (Beto 90), Rui Jorge, Rochemback, Moutinho, Liedson (Rodrigo Tello 77), Rogerio, Viana. Unused subs: Nélson; Carlos Martins, Marius Niculae, Miguel Garcia.
Referee: Stefano Farina, Italy.
Bookings
Middlesbrough: Parnaby 80, foul.
Sporting Lisbon: None.
Attendance: 23,739
Conditions: Cool, dry and still

Thursday March 17 2005

Venue: Jose Alvalade Stadium
Result: **Sporting Lisbon 1 Middlesbrough 0**
Goalscorer: Pedro Barbosa 89.
Teams
Sporting Lisbon: Ricardo; Hugo (Douala 34), Barbosa (Capt.) (Martins 90), Enakarhire, Beto, Rui Jorge, Sa Pinto, Moutinho, Liedson (Niculae 87), Rogerio, Viana. Unused subs: Nélson (gk); Garcia, Tello, Sergio.
Middlesbrough: Schwarzer; McMahon (Graham 67), Riggott, Southgate, Queudrue, Parnaby (Wheater 90), Doriva (Johnson 79), Zenden, Downing, Nemeth, Job. Unused subs: Jones (gk); Cooper, Taylor, Kennedy.
Referee: Eric Poulat, France.
Bookings
Sporting Lisbon: Niculae 87, ungentlemanly conduct.
Middlesbrough: None
Attendance: 21,217
Conditions: Warm and pleasant

Thursday September 15 2005

Venue:	Riverside Stadium
Result:	**Middlesbrough 2 Xanthi 0**
Goalscorers:	Boateng 28, Paviot og 82.

Teams

Middlesbrough: Schwarzer; Xavier, Ehiogu, Bates, Pogatetz, Parlour (Morrison 74), Boateng, Doriva, Johnson (Queudrue 59), Maccarone (Yakubu 74), Viduka. Unused subs: Jones (gk); Southgate, Kennedy, Graham.

Xanthi: Pizanowski; Papadimitrou, Emerson, Luciano, Labriakos, Sikov, Paviot (Kazakis 87), Antzas, Chiquinho, Maghradze (Cozalves 77), Torosidis (Quintana 67). Unused subs: Anastasopoulos (gk); Zapropoulos, Carabas, Lafata.

Referee:	Steffan Messner, Austria.

Bookings

Middlesbrough:	Bates 65, handball.
Xanthi:	None
Attendance:	14,191
Conditions:	Cool and breezy.

Thursday September 29 2005

Venue:	Skoda Xanthi Stadium
Result:	**Xanthi 0 Middlesbrough 0**

Teams

Xanthi: Pizanowski; Papadimitrou, Emerson, Luciano, Labriakos, Sikov, Paviot, Antzas, Chiquinho (Leo Mineiro 60), Maghradze (Garpozis 68), Torosidis (Kazakis 46). Unused subs: Anastasopoulos (gk); Zapropoulos, Carabas, Lafata.

Middlesbrough: Jones; Xavier, Riggott, Southgate (Capt), Pogatetz, Morrison, Doriva, Boateng, Queudrue (Parnaby 77), Hasselbaink (Yakubu 70), Maccarone (Nemeth 70). Unused subs: Knight, Bates, Mendieta, Johnson.

Referee:	Knut Kircher. Germany.

Bookings

Xanthi:	Luciano, 74, foul on Riggott
Middlesbrough:	Queudrue, 46, foul on Chiquino; Jones, 70, time-wasting
Attendance :	5,013
Conditions:	Mild and pleasant

Thursday October 20 2005

Venue: Hardturm Stadium
Result: **Grasshoppers 0 Middlesbrough 1**
Goalscorer: Hasselbaink 9.
Teams
Grasshoppers: Coltorti; Stepanovs, Mitreski, Jaggy, Chihab, Cabanas, Dos Santos,
                     Renggli (Salatic 87), Rogerio, Eduardo, Sutter. Unused subs: Jehle
                     (gk); Schwegler, Hurlimann, Denicola, Toure, Lutolf.
Middlesbrough: Schwarzer; Parnaby, Riggott, Southgate (Capt), Pogatetz, Mendieta
                     (Queudrue 78), Boateng, Doriva, Nemeth (Morrison 66), Viduka
                     (Yakubu, 84), Hasselbaink. Unused subs: Jones (gk); Bates,
                     Maccarone, A Johnson.
Referee: Espen Berntsen, Norway.
Bookings
Grasshoppers: None
Middlesbrough: Pogatetz 64, foul on Chihab; Nemeth 67, time wasting.
Attendance: 8,500
Conditions: Clear, cool and quite sharp.

Thursday November 3 2005

Venue: Riverside Stadium
Result: **Middlesbrough 3 Dnipro 0**
Goalscorers: Yakubu 35, Viduka 50, 55
Teams
Middlesbrough: Schwarzer (Capt.); Bates, Riggott, Queudrue, Parnaby, Doriva,
                     Mendieta (Kennedy 59), Morrison, Pogatetz, Yakubu (Maccarone
                     56), Viduka (Nemeth 64). Unused subs: Jones (gk); Boateng,
                     Johnson, Hasselbaink.
Dnipro: Kusliy; Yezerskiy, Radchenko, Kostyshyn, Shershun, Rusol
                     (Lysytskiy 58), Shelayev, Semochko, Mykhaylenko (Capt.) (Motuz
                     65), Nazarenko, Rykun. Unused subs: Kernozenko (gk);
                     Melaschenko, Kornilenko, Bidnenko, Kravchenko.
Referee: Bertrand Layec. France.
Bookings
Middlesbrough: None
Dnipro: Shershun 90, dissent.
Attendance: 12,953
Conditions: Cool, still, at pitch level, and dry.

Thursday November 24 2005

Venue: Alkmaarderhout Stadium
Result: **AZ Alkmaar 0 Middlesbrough 0**
Teams
AZ Alkmaar: Timmer; Jaliens, Mathijsen, De Cler, Landzaat (Capt.), Arveladze (Koevermans 77), Van Galen, Perez, Sektioui (Meerdink 60), Steinsson, Schaars. Unused subs: Buskermolen, Huysegems, Vlaar, Zwarthoed, Ramzi.
Middlesbrough: Jones; Bates, Riggott, Ehiogu, Pogatetz, Doriva, Morrison (Parnaby 63), Boateng, Nemeth (Queudrue 74), Hasselbaink (Capt.), Viduka (Yakubu 63). Unused subs: Knight (gk); Southgate, Maccarone, Johnson.
Referee: Gianluca Paparesta, Italy.
Bookings
AZ Alkmaar: Schaars 23, foul on Boateng; Steinsson 71, foul on Boateng.
Middlesbrough: Hasselbaink 30, throwing ball away; Pogatetz 49, foul on Steinsson; Boateng 57, foul on Steinsson.
Attendance: 8,461
Conditions: Pouring rain, cold.

Thursday December 15 2005

Venue: Riverside Stadium
Result: **Middlesbrough 2 Litex Lovech 0**
Goalscorer: Maccarone 80, 86
Teams
Middlesbrough: Jones; Bates, Riggott, Ehiogu, Queudrue, Morrison, Doriva, Kennedy, Johnson, Hasselbaink (Cattermole 83), Maccarone. Unused subs: Schwarzer (gk); Southgate, Wheater, Boateng, Viduka, Yakubu.
Litex Lovech: Vutov; Palankov (Kirilov 77), Cichero, Venkov, Caillet, Genchev, Sandrinho (Hazorov 87), Jelenkovic (Capt.), Zlatinov (Lyubenov 74), Berberovic, Novakovic. Unused subs: Todorov (gk); Zhelev, Manolev, Zanev.
Referee: Mr S Gumienny, Belgium.
Bookings
Middlesbrough: Cattermole 89, foul on Caillet.
Litex Lovech: Venkov 40, foul on Morrison; Berberovic 59, foul on Queudrue.
Attendance: 9,436
Conditions: Mild and still

Thursday February 16 2006

Venue:	Gottlieb-Daimler Stadium
Result:	**VfB Stuttgart 1 Middlesbrough 2**
Goalscorers:	Hasselbaink 19, Parnaby 46, Ljuboja 88

Teams

VfB Stuttgart: Hildebrand; Stranzl (Beck 46), Meira, Gerber, Delpierre, Meissner (Gentner 77), Hitzlsperger (Gomez 63), Soldo (Capt.), Gronkjaer, Tomasson, Ljuboja. Unused subs: Heinen (gk); Babbel, Magnin, Tiffert.

Middlesbrough: Schwarzer; Davies, Riggott, Southgate (Capt.), Pogatetz, Parnaby, Boateng (Kennedy 78), Doriva, Rochemback, Downing (Johnson 70), Hasselbaink (Yakubu 82). Unused subs: Jones (gk); McMahon, Bates, Taylor.

Referee: Alain Hamer, Luxembourg.

Bookings

VfB Stuttgart: Hitzlsperger 33, foul on Boateng; Meira 90, kicking the ball away.

Middlesbrough: Pogatetz 21, foul on Gronkjaer; Davies 65, foul on Gerber.

Attendance:	21,000
Conditions:	Cold and heavy rain.

Thursday February 23 2006

Venue:	Riverside Stadium
Result:	**Middlesbrough 0 VfB Stuttgart 1**
Goalscorer:	Tiffert 13

Teams

Middlesbrough: Schwarzer; Davies, Riggott, Southgate (Capt.), Queudrue, Parnaby, Mendieta (Ehiogu 85), Boateng, Cattermole, Downing (Taylor 90), Hasselbaink (Yakubu 85). Unused subs: Jones (gk); McMahon, Maccarone, Viduka.

VfB Stuttgart: Hildebrand; Hinkel, Babbel, Delpierre, Gentner, Meissner (Cacau 75), Tiffert, Soldo (Capt.), Gronkjaer (Gomez 64), Magnin (Hitzlsperger 80), Ljuboja. Unused subs: Heinen (gk); Gerber, Carevic, Beck.

Referee: Eric Braamhaar, Holland.

Bookings

Middlesbrough: Boateng 31, foul; Mendieta 51, foul; Cattermole 90, playing on when offside.

VfB Stuttgart: Tiffert 52, foul.

Attendance:	24,018
Conditions:	Cold, windy with soaking, swirling, heavy drizzle.

Thursday March 9 2006

Venue: Riverside Stadium
Result: **Middlesbrough 1 AS Roma 0**
Goalscorer: Yakubu 12 (pen).
Teams
Middlesbrough: Schwarzer; Davies, Riggott, Southgate (Capt), Pogatetz, Mendieta, Boateng, Cattermole, Downing (Queudrue 90), Hasselbaink, Yakubu (Viduka 80). Unused subs: Jones (gk); McMahon, Parlour, Doriva, Maccarone.
AS Roma: Curci; Pannucci, Mexes, Kuffour, Cufre, Taddei (Okaka 60), Dacourt (Aquilani 83), Kharja, Tommasi (Capt.) (Alvarez 73), Perrotta, Mancini. Unused subs: Pipolo (gk); Bovo, Chivu, Rosi.
Referee: Alain Sars. France.
Bookings
Middlesbrough: Riggott 71, foul on Okaka.
AS Roma: Perrotta 41, foul on Yakubu; Mexes 88, foul on Viduka.
Attendance: 25,354
Conditions: Damp, still and occasional rain.

Wednesday March 15 2006

Venue: Stadio Olimpico
Result: **AS Roma 2 Middlesbrough 1**
Goalscorers: Hasselbaink 32, Mancini 42, 65 (pen).
Teams
AS Roma: Curci; Bovo, Mexes, Kuffour, Chivu (Pannucci 85), Taddei, Dacourt (Okaka 63), De Rossi, Alvarez (Aquilani 71), Perrotta, Mancini. Unused subs: Eleftheropoulos (gk); Kharja, Cufre, Rosi.
Middlesbrough: Schwarzer; Davies (Queudrue 46), Riggott, Southgate (Capt), Pogatetz, Mendieta, Boateng, Cattermole, Downing, Hasselbaink, Yakubu (Parlour 58). Unused subs: Jones (gk); Ehiogu, Doriva, Viduka, Maccarone.
Referee: Tom Henning Ovrebo. Norway.
Sent-off: Mexes yellow card 30, retaliation, and 90, foul on Downing
Bookings
AS Roma: Mancini 31, elbow on Mendieta; Bovo 85, retaliation.
Middlesbrough: Cattermole 14, kicking the ball away; Boateng 30, foul on Perrotta; Pogatetz 85, foul on Bovo.
Attendance: 32,642
Conditions: Clear and cool

Thursday March 30 2006

Venue: St Jakob Park
Result: **FC Basel 2 Middlesbrough 0**
Goalscorers: Delgado 42, Degen 45.
Teams
FC Basel: Zuberbuhler; Zanni, Majstorovic, Smiljanic, Berner, Ba, Delgado, Petric (Ergic 85), Degen, Sterjovski (Chipperfield 64), Eduardo. Unused subs: Crayton (gk); Quennoz, Kuzmanovic, Kulaksizoglu, Rakitic.
Middlesbrough: Schwarzer; Parnaby, Riggott (Capt.), Pogatetz (Ehiogu 68), Queudrue, Mendieta (Rochemback 74), Parlour, Doriva, Downing, Hasselbaink (Yakubu 74), Viduka. Unused subs: Jones (gk); Davies, Morrison, Taylor.
Referee: Roberto Rosetti, Italy
Bookings
FC Basel: Degen 28, diving; Majstorovic 40, foul on Viduka.
Middlesbrough: Downing 52, kicking the ball away; Riggott 76, foul on Delgado.
Attendance: 23,639
Conditions: Relatively mild, fine, soaking rain.

Thursday April 6 2006

Venue: Riverside Stadium
Result: **Middlesbrough 4 FC Basel 1**
Goalscorers: Eduardo 22, Viduka 33, 56, Hasselbaink 78, Maccarone 90
Teams
Middlesbrough: Schwarzer; Parnaby, Riggott, Southgate, Queudrue (Maccarone 66), Morrison (Hasselbaink 46), Boateng, Rochemback, Downing, Yakubu (Taylor 90), Viduka. Unused subs: Jones (gk); Davies, Ehiogu, Doriva.
FC Basel: Zuberbuhler; Zanni, Majstorovic, Smiljanic, Berner, Ba, Delgado (Ergic 70), Petric, Degen (Chipperfield 60), Sterjovski (Quennoz 85), Eduardo. Unused subs: Crayton (gk); Kulaksizoglu, Rakitic.
Referee: Iouri Baskakov, Russia.
Sent-off: Majstorovic yellow card 51, foul on Hasselbaink and 73, slapping Boateng.
Bookings
Middlesbrough: Riggott 24, foul on Petric; Parnaby 44, foul on Berner; Maccarone 90, taking his shirt off to celebrate.
FC Basel: Smiljanic 90, foul.
Attendance: 24,521
Conditions: Fine, cool with a gentle breeze.

Thursday April 20 2006

Venue: Lia Manoliu Stadium
Result: **Steaua Bucharest 1 Middlesbrough 0**
Goalscorer: Dica 29
Teams
Steaua Bucharest: Carlos; Goian, Ogararu, Ghionea, Radoi, Marin, Bostina, Dica,
      Paraschiv (Lovin 86), Oprita (Cristea 89), Nicolita. Unused subs:
      Cernea (gk); Balan, Cristocea, Nesu, Baciu.
Middlesbrough: Schwarzer; Parnaby, Bates, Ehiogu (Capt.), Queudrue, Morrison
      (Parlour 70), Boateng, Rochemback, Downing, Hasselbaink,
      Yakubu (Maccarone 70). Unused subs: Jones (gk); Wheater, Taylor,
      Doriva, Christie.
Referee: Alan Hamer. Luxembourg.
Bookings
Steaua Bucharest: Paraschiv 32, foul on Queudrue; Goian 38, foul on Yakubu;
      Nicolita 40, foul on Queudrue; Marin 88, foul on Maccarone.
Middlesbrough: Schwarzer 75, time-wasting; Parlour 89, foul on Marin.
Attendance: 41,000
Conditions: Cool and dry.

Thursday April 27 2006

Venue: Riverside Stadium
Result: **Middlesbrough 4 Steaua Bucharest 2**
Goalscorers: Dica 16, Goian 23, Maccarone 33, Viduka 64, Riggott 72,
      Maccarone 90.
Teams
Middlesbrough: Jones; Riggott, Southgate (Maccarone 25), Queudrue, Boateng,
      Parnaby, Rochemback, Downing, Taylor (Yakubu 55), Viduka,
      Hasselbaink (Ehiogu 89). Unused subs: Knight (gk); Bates,
      Cattermole, Parlour.
Steaua Bucharest: Carlos; Goian, Ogararu, Ghionea, Radoi, Marin, Bostina (Nesu
      86), Dica, Lovin, Oprita (Baciu 81), Iacob (Balan 65). Unused
      subs: Cernea (gk); Simion, Cristocea, Cristea.
Referee: Lubos Michel, Slovakia.
Bookings
Middlesbrough: Boateng 59, foul on Radoi; Hasselbaink 60, diving.
Steaua Bucharest: Dica 67, handball; Balan 74, foul on Yakubu; Lovin 74, kicking the
      ball away.
Attendance: 34,622
Conditions: Mild with a light breeze.

Wednesday May 10 2006

Venue:	PSV Stadion
Result:	**Middlesbrough 0 Sevilla 4**
Goalscorers:	Luis Fabiano 26, Maresca 78, 84, Kanoute 89
Teams	
Middlesbrough:	Schwarzer; Parnaby, Riggott, Southgate (Capt.), Queudrue (Yakubu 70), Morrison (Maccarone 46), Boateng, Rochemback, Downing, Hasselbaink, Viduka (Cattermole 85). Unused subs: Jones (gk); Ehiogu, Bates, Parlour.
Seville:	Palop; Navarro (Capt.), David, Daniel Alves, Escude, Saviola (Kanoute 46), Luis Fabiano (Renato 72), Jesus Navas, Adriano (Puerta 85), Marti, Maresca. Unused subs: Notario (gk); Aitor Ocio, Fernando Sales, Kepa.
Referee:	Herbert Fandel, Germany.
Bookings	
Middlesbrough:	Rochemback 82, foul on Kanoute.
Seville:	Alves 52, foul on Downing; Escude 80, time wasting; Maresca 84, taking his shirt off to celebrate a goal.
Attendance:	36,500
Conditions:	Very warm after a hot sunny day.

Compiled by
Gordon Cox

OFFICIAL SPONSOR OF THE ROAD TO EINDHOVEN

AND OF THE CENTURY FM BORO COMMENTARY MAN OF THE MATCH

- MIDDLESBROUGH
- DARLINGTON
- HARTLEPOOL
- REDCAR

01642 888711

ALWAYS SUPPORTING
THE BORO

BOX CLOTHING